Celadon Blues

Robert Tichane

**Previously published as *Those Celadon Blues*.
Now back in print with an added color section.**

Previously published as Those Celadon Blues, 1978, 1983 under ISBN 0-914267-03-5
Now back in print with an added color section.

Published by

700 East State St., Iola, WI 54990-0001
Telephone 715-445-2214
www.krause.com

Please, call or write us for our free catalog of publications. Our toll-free number to place an order or obtain a free
catalog is 800-258-0929 or please use our regular business telephone 715-445-2214 for editorial comment and
further information.

Manufactured in the United States of America

Library of Congress Cataloging-in-Publication Data
Tichane, Robert
Celadon blues
ISBN: 0-87341-667-8

1. Glaze   2. Pottery   3. Title

98-87289
CIP

Frontispiece—Kiln waster from Lung-ch'uan. Courtesy of the Metropolitan Museum of Art,
Gift of Mrs. Samuel T. Peters, 1926.
26.292.80

To
MARGENE

CONTENTS

FOREWORD

There is no area in the ceramic field which holds more mystery or intrigue than the pottery produced by the ancient Chinese potters. In particular, the glazes produced during the Sung Dynasty (960-1279AD) are especially rich, exotic and mysterious. Also they are most difficult to reproduce.

It is fortunate that the author, an expert analyst, also has a keen interest in Sung glazes. What was the secret of these ancient potters which resulted in glazes of such richness and beauty? Why were they seldom duplicated?

By his application of several modern and powerful analytical techniques together with untold hours of work in his studio, he has uncovered these secrets and techniques.

In doing so he has, by the application of scientific methods, contributed not only to the understanding of Sung glazes but also to the important roles which glaze-body interaction, raw materials, kiln atmosphere and phase separation play in glaze behavior.

Both the ceramic artist and scientist are fortunate that he has chosen to publish the results of his work.

W. G. Lawrence, Dean
NYS College of Ceramics
at Alfred University

CELADON

. . . . the color produced in reduced feldspathic glazes by low percentages of iron. Celadons are usually soft yellow-green to blue-green colors because of contamination by titania. In the absence of titania, blues can be obtained which approach:

"The blue of the sky
 as seen through rifts in the clouds
 after a rain."

CHAPTER 1

INTRODUCTION

This work originated because of a desire to duplicate one Kuan bowl. The beauty of this ware as illustrated in the collection of the National Palace Museum was so outstanding, that one had to be captivated by it. Also it seemed within the realm of possibility for an average potter to make such a piece. The size was modest, the shape was simple and the glaze was merely a crackled celadon.

Now, nearly 10 years and a few thousand pots later I have come to the conclusion that while Kuan bowls are small in size and simple in shape, there is no such thing as a "mere" celadon glaze.

Eventually, the project broadened in scope and in the course of pursuing the Kuan glaze several other Sung dynasty wares were attempted because they all seemed to be related. As the project expanded into the field of Sung glazes in general, the techniques began to expand too. Instead of just using cut-and-try synthesis, the possibility of using a little science emerged.

The biggest advance took place when Margaret Medley very kindly provided sherds of Chun and Yueh bowls. The chance to examine these Sung glazes and bodies closely, advanced the work by a quantum jump. Margaret also provided Kuan sherds, a Temmoku sample, and additional Yueh sherds, as well as a tremendous amount of useful advice.

The sherds were first examined visually, then in cross section by optical microscopy, and finally by Scanning Electron Microscopy (SEM) and Energy Dispersive X-Ray Analysis (EDXR). The ability to examine sherds by SEM and EDXR at the Corning Glass Works laboratory has been a great help in learning about these ceramics.

Finally, after collecting reams of information about Sung ceramics I decided to put the data into permanent form. Some of this work has been reported at annual meetings of The American Ceramic Society, but it has not appeared in print before.

A strong word of warning should be made to those readers who expect to use this as a recipe book for making Sung glazes. It won't take you 10 years to make a glaze after reading this book, but it won't happen after 10 pages and 10 attempts either. The glazes themselves are not complex chemically, but the techniques are something that have to be learned slowly. One must be patient in order to make Sung ware. You must try, and adjust, then retry, and readjust. I have found for example, that after several months of not making Chun glazes, it will take me a week or a month of constant trying to get back into a successful groove again. And this is with the advantage of having known recipes, known raw materials and a well-controlled kiln.

WHY SUNG?

The question should be asked, "Why write a book about Sung Glazes? Why not write a book about all Chinese glazes, about T'ang glazes, or Ming glazes, or Ch'ing glazes?"

The answer is: glazes more recent than Sung are adequately covered in modern glaze books such as "Ceramic Glazes" by Parmelee. Ming and Ch'ing glazes are thin, feldspathic or lead types that are well within the command of modern ceramists.

As for pre-Sung glazes, the lead types of the T'ang dynasty and before are simple glazes that can be formulated readily today, while Han and previous ash glazes are both crude and simple.

Sung glazes on the other hand are unique. The particular glazes represented in this book have never been made on a large scale either before or after the Sung era. Occasionally potters have been entranced by the beauty of a Sung glaze and have duplicated it as a special feat, but no continuous manufacture of Sung type ware has been carried out since 1300 AD. This is not accidental, because Sung glazes are rather fussy and involve a lot of care and even accidents.

Therefore the next question is: "Why bother, if these glazes are so difficult to make?" But that query is easy to answer. Sung glazes are really exotic! They were probably intended to look like jade, and they not only resemble it, they even look better than jade on occasion.

THE FACTORS

There were four essential ingredients in this investigation of Sung ceramics.

Number one was the availability of authentic Sung sherds. Obviously if you don't know what the real thing looks like, you can't duplicate it.

Second was the possibility of using Scanning Electron Microscopy and Energy Dispersive X-Ray analysis to evaluate the sherds. Again, one can have all the sherds in the world, but if you have no way to classify and identify them, they are not useful.

Third was the capability of making hundreds of samples to prove and disprove the many concepts of how Sung ceramics were originally made.

Finally, the most useful factor was help from the past. The valuable assistance provided by friends, historians, ceramicists, chemists, etc. was irreplaceable. And, where would one be without the literature as a background, as a base on which to build one more step.

THE SHERDS

Sherds are the keystone to this book. Some initial attempts were made at formulating Chinese-like celadons from pictures and descriptions, but the effects were variable and generally poor. On the other hand once work started with sherds, it was like taking an examination with a book open.

Margaret Medley gave me a generous start by providing Chun and Yueh sherds from the Percival David Collection. In addition, Margaret's probing questions and thoughtful suggestions on glaze and body problems were a great source of inspiration. Later she also provided Kuan, Chien, and additional Yueh pieces that kept the Sung research going.

From another source I received a Chien sherd that had been collected by James Plumer in Fukien province.

A slide of a Kuan thin-section was loaned by Tom Chase at the Freer Gallery. And sherds and bowls were examined at the Metropolitan Museum of Art thanks to Sue Valenstein.

A big step forward occurred at the Ostasiatiske Museet with the help of Jan Wirgin and Bo Gyllensvard. There I was allowed to examine the Palmgren sherds and to take samples for microscopic examination. These included 5 Lung-ch'uan types, 2 Kuan, a Northern celadon, a Chun, a Ch'ing-pai, a Ting type, and a white Sung piece.

ACKNOWLEDGEMENTS

In back of every book is a long trail of generous people who have given time, advice, and assistance of various kinds. These are the co-authors. The fellow on the title page is really just an editor or collector. Here are some of the contributors to this book;

Bob Garrett — who got me started quickly and firmly in the ceramics game.

Paul Soldner — showed me how to make my own backyard kiln.

Dan Rhodes — put it all together in one picture.

W. G. Lawrence — for encouragement both before and after reading the manuscript.

Henry Sereno — showed me how to glaze and fire correctly.

Val Cushing — who provided a special insight into Chien coloration.

Rick St. John — did the same for throwing.

Wally Higgins — made the Northern celadon bowl come true.

Margaret Medley — provided sherds and good advice.

Fred Bickford — for making the test kiln possible.

A. A. Erickson — gave freely of his glass melting experience

Father Daniel — provided ash and Temmoku information

Bob Brill — who introduced me to museums and their staffs.

Tom Chase — showed me the Freer collection and a Kuan sherd.

John Pope — provided a most useful Chien sherd.

Jean Lee — started me on a one-bowl Sung ceramic collection.

Ed Korda and Jean Williams — allowed me the opportunity to work with the scanning electron microscope.

Len Pruden — who showed me how to work with the SEM and who kept it going.

Patty Proctor — Made the great translation of Chinese research on Sung ceramics.

Pam Koush — helped me puzzle out the Chun glaze mystery.

Christine Rousseau — got me trying to make real Sung pots.

Sue Valenstein — inspired me and taught me the details of Sung ceramic history.

Jan Wirgin — set up my trip to the Ostasiatiske Museet.

Bo Gyllensvard — allowed me to study and sample the Palmgren collection.

Ernie King — my one local contact who would talk to me about Chinese ceramics.

Harold Bopp - gave me the benefit of his experience at Rookwood Pottery.

Claude Davis — a loyal co-worker, always willing to help with advice.

Dozens of friends whom I never met, but who wrote about their ceramic studies so that we really needed no introduction. People like: Hetherington, Palmgren, Sundius, Steger, Hobson, David, Bushell, Seger, Plumer, plus countless un-named Chinese potters and writers. I feel like I know them all intimately.

Special thanks are due to "The New York State Institute for Glaze Research" for the grant which makes this publication possible.

Mining the Stone.

CHAPTER 2

THE LITERATURE

The best part about "The Literature" is that almost everything is covered there somewhere. If you look long enough, hard enough, far enough, you can find any situation defined, any glaze analyzed, any technique described.

The hard part about the literature is that pieces you may need most are: the farthest dispersed; are out-of-print; can only be found in Japanese; are incorrectly translated; or are only available two months after your deadline. But in particular we are going to reserve places in the deepest recesses of Hades for those gentle men and women who refer us to: (1) Personal Communication, and (2) To Be Published!

However, in all seriousness, at least 90% of the information you may need on ceramic subjects can be readily found in available literature. You must decide though, how to start the ball rolling. Since you currently have a copy of this book, you must already have available to you — a bookstore, a friend, or a library.

Everyone should start their own collection of ceramic literature, for friends have the unpleasant habit of moving, and libraries have been known to thoughtlessly loan essential books to other people at a critical moment. Your personal library doesn't have to be too large, six appropriate volumes may be enough, although 100 have been known to be just one short.

Where you live will have a great influence on where you buy your books, but your local public library can help you discover this. Even in the farthest reaches of central South Dakota, the U.S. mail is available. For recent books on Chinese ceramics you can obtain a catalog from the Paragon bookstore in New York City (14 East 38th St. 10016). For out of print books you can advertise in search magazines recommended by your local library. For technical articles, a trip to the nearest State College library will do the trick, or have your local public library send for copies. Then again, when you take your next vacation, plan to visit and spend a day at some great ceramic or Chinese library like Alfred U. or the Cornell U. Wason collection.

It is practical to keep a list of books and journals you need to read, then one day when you have nothing inspiring to do, take a special trip to a library and look everything up at once.

You should collect at least a skeleton library of your own, though, always aiming at a basic collection of classics. I have 6-12 tooks that are referred to again and again, with perhaps another 50 that are helpful once in awhile. Most of these books were no more expensive than a restaurant dinner, or a tankful of gas. Occasionally a book is exhorbitantly priced, but if it is as valuable as "Sung Sherds" has been to me, it is a pearl of great value.

REFERENCES

These books have been the most important for this work. There may be a few missing, but not many because friends kept me posted when good books came along. The special areas of interest covered here are: Sung ceramics, celadons, and ceramic techniques.

Sung Sherds — Palmgren, Sundius, & Steger — Stockholm — 1963.

Chinese Ceramic Glazes — Hetherington A.L. — Commonwealth — 1948.

Ching-te Chen T'ao Lu-Sayer G.R. — Routledge — 1951.

Chinese Celadon Wares — Gompertz G.M. — Faber — 1958.

A Handbook of Chinese Ceramics — Valenstein S. — MMA — 1975.

Oriental Ceramic Art — Bushell S.W. — Appletons — 1899.

Chinese Pottery and Porcelain — Hobson R.L. — Dover — 1976.

The Ceramic Art of China — Honey W.B. — Faber — 1945.

Early Ming Wares — Brankston A.D. — Paragon — 1970 (reprint).

The Chinese Potter — Medley M. — Oxford — 1976.

Temmoku — Plumer J.M. — Tokyo — 1972.

Ceramic Science — Lawrence W.G. — Chilton — 1972.

Industrial Ceramics — Singer F. & Singer S. — Chem. Pub. — 1963.

The Collected Writings of H.A. Seger — Chem. Pub. — 1902.

Ceramic Glazes — Parmelee & Harman — Cahners — 1973.

Clay and Glazes for the Potter — Rhodes D. — Chilton — 1973.

Kilns — Rhodes D. — Chilton — 1973.

Far Eastern Ceramic Bulletin

Transactions of the Oriental Ceramic Society — London

CHINESE

DYNASTIC

CHRONOLOGY

```
SHANG  .....................  1523-1028 BC
CHOU ......................  1027- 256 BC
HAN  ......................  206 BC-220 AD
SIX DYNASTIES  ..............  220 - 589 AD
T'ANG  ....................  618 - 906 AD
FIVE DYNASTIES  ............  907 - 960 AD
SUNG  ......................  960-1279 AD
YUAN  .....................  1279-1368 AD
MING  .....................  1368-1644 AD
CH'ING  ...................  1644-1912 AD
```

CHAPTER 3

CHINESE CERAMIC HISTORY

This chapter is difficult to write with any easy conscience because it is obviously not possible to discuss the ceramic history of billions of people over a period of thousands of years in something like a few pages. However, an attempt is necessary in order to place Sung clay products in perspective with regard to historical Chinese ceramics.

For starters, there has never been a logical flow in the development of Chinese ceramics over the course of years. Certain glaze types, body types, and designs have cropped up, only to disappear and then reappear later. This cyclical occurrence and disappearance has been particularly noteworthy in regard to lead glazes and in regard to porcelain bodies.

SHANG

Starting with the Shang dynasty (1500-1000 BC), it is possible to find the antecedents of porcelain ware, because even at that early age stoneware-like ceramics were being made (Figure 3.1).

Figure 3.1. Stoneware jar of the Shang dynasty.

Courtesy: The Nelson-Atkins Museum of Art, Kansas City, Missouri.
Purchase: Nelson Trust. (34-253)

The significance of this development is that high firing temperatures (1200°C.) were being used in China 2-3000 years before their use in Europe. One must remember however, that **most** of the ceramics at this time were made of earthenware.

CHOU

Early surface finishes were of several types: one involved burnishing of the clay to give it a gloss; another utilized application of pigments (frequently iron oxides) to give color; and still another used a form of crude glaze for either gloss, impermeability, or color. In the Chou dynasty (1027-256 BC) are found two kinds of fired ceramic glazes, a yellowish ash-type (figure 3.2), and a green lead glaze (Figure 3.3).

Figure 3.2. Stoneware Chou kettle with yellowish glaze.

Courtesy of the Ashmolean Museum, Oxford.

Figure 3.3. Earthenware Chou jar with green lead glaze.

Courtesy: The Nelson-Atkins Museum of Art, Kansas City, Missouri. Purchase: Nelson Trust. (34-254)

15

HAN

During the Han dynasty (206 BC-220 AD), which roughly paralleled the Roman empire, many solid advances in glaze technique can be observed. For one thing, lead glazes became quite common and many funerary vessels have survived (Figure 3.4). Stoneware objects were also more frequent and often were glazed on their upper portions with ash-type glazes (Figure 3.5). These ash glazes of Chou and Han would eventually give rise to celadon types in later periods.

Figure 3.4. Green, lead-glazed
Han funerary jar.

Figure 3.5. Han stoneware jar
with green, ash-type glaze.

17

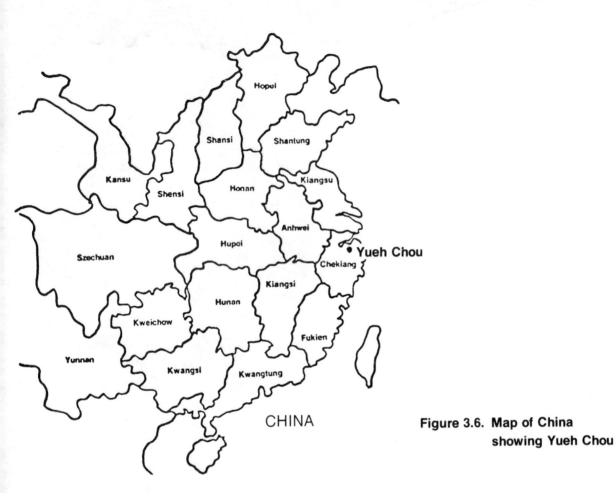

Figure 3.6. Map of China
showing Yueh Chou

SIX DYNASTIES

The Six Dynasties era is remarkable for the origin of Yueh ware. Yueh ceramics, named for an administrative city in Chekiang province (Figure 3.6) spanned a period of several hundred years. The 'type' ware had a thin celadon glaze on a dense grey body with colors varying from yellow-brown to clear greens. With the progression of time from early Six Dynasties to the Sung dynasty, the bodies became finer in texture and lighter in color, and the glaze color tended towards purer greens.

Other ceramic trends in the Six Dynasties period involved lead glazes and pale bodies. The first multi-colored lead glazed ceramics appeared, with yellow, green, and brown colors (low-iron, copper, and high-iron content), and, the appearance of near-white ceramics (in both low-fired and high-fired types) occurred.

Figure 3.7. T'ang porcelain ewer with phoenix head.

T'ANG

The T'ang dynasty seemed to be noteworthy in all fields and ceramics was no exception. Now we see true porcelain pieces, multi-colored lead glazed ware, and superb celadons. The porcelain-like pieces are certainly not common in this dynasty, but the challenge was met and conquered (Figure 3.7).

Figure 3.8 Lead-glazed horse T'ang dynasty. 30″ high.

The occurrence of cobalt blue color in lead-glazed pieces is quite frequent and we see marvelously sculpted figures of all kinds (Figure 3.8) with lead glazes in green(copper), yellow(iron), blue(cobalt), and brown(iron).

**Figure 3.9. Yueh ware,
T'ang dynasty.**

Yueh celadons were splendid at this time (Figure 3.9), due in part to the remarkable carving, and in part to the fine bodies and glazes. Some T'ang ware was exported with pieces being found as far afield as Iraq and Iran.

SUNG

The Sung dynasty was my area of concentration simply because it was the source of a great number of unusual glazes. The Chinese ash and lead glazes that were common until now, have also appeared in other civilizations, and their fabrication was rather straight forward. But Sung glazes in most cases were quite different and in fact have never been widely duplicated. Additionally, the Sung glazes are so beautiful that they are definitely worth the task of rediscovery.

The several chapters following this one will describe individual Sung glazes in detail, but here is a brief overview of them in general.

In north China, during the Sung dynasty, are found the splendidly decorated Tz'u-chou ceramics (Figure 3.10), with great artistry displayed in rather simple glazes and slips.

Courtesy: The Nelson-Atkins Museum of Art, Kansas City, Missouri. Purchase: Nelson Trust. (70-3)

Figure 3.10. Sung Tz'u-chou vase.

Another northern ware is the Northern celadon (Figure 3.11), which just "cries out" to be compared with Yueh ware. The beautifully carved and molded Northern celadon ceramics are really a tribute to artistic technique in which the glaze has just a secondary role.

Figure 3.12. Ting plate of the Sung dynasty.

The same can be said for Ting pieces (Figure 3.12). They have gorgeous decorations with a rather modest cream-colored or ivory glaze. A point of interest about Ting ware is that some of the pieces were made for the Imperial household.

25

Figure 3.13. A Sung Chun plate glazed in blue celadon with copper splashes.

Chun ware, also made in north China, represents a class of ceramics where the glaze is the most important attribute of the piece (Figure 3.13). The shapes are simple, the sizes are unpretentious, and until later dynasties there was no carved or molded decoration. The glaze, however, was colorful and thick, and had a tactile stone-like finish.

Courtesy of the Cleveland Museum of Art, Purchase, John L. Severance Fund.

Figure 3.14 Ju dish of the Sung dynasty.

Two types of Sung ware were made exclusively for the imperial household. Ju was reportedly made only from 1107-1127 AD and while the volume represented in collections is very small, the beautiful blue-green crackled glaze and simple shapes make it an outstanding example of the Sung potter's craft (Figure 3.14).

Courtesy of the Percival David Foundation of Chinese Art.

Figure 3.15. Southern Sung Kuan bowl.

Kuan, the other imperial ware, was reportedly made in both northern and southern China, although specific kiln sites have not been found in the north as yet. Kuan has a pale blue, crackled glaze that is very thick and jade-like (Figure 3.15). Its most remarkable feature though, is a thin body of approximately the same thickness as the heavy glaze.

Figure 3.16. Export Lung-ch'uan ware excavated in the Philippines.

Some ware found in Chekiang province was a continuation of the Yueh tradition, but this passed from the scene in the Sung dynasty. In the same period there was a rise in the production of Lung-ch'uan-type celadons. The location for Lung-ch'uan production was in southern Chekiang province in the mountainous region close to Fukien. The finest examples of Lung-ch'uan celadons (Kinuta in particular) are different from Yueh in having thicker glazes and in being underfired (Figure 3.16).

Figure 3.17. Sung Ch'ing-pai stem cup sherd in sagger. Ching-te Chen, 1981.

Ch'ing-pai is a transition glaze, marking the change from thick Sung glazes to the thinner Ming types. Ch'ing-pai was carved, in the tradition of Yueh, Northern celadons and Ting ware. But it was coated with a thin, pale blue glaze (Figure 3.17).

Figure 3.18. Yuan vase with blue-and-white decoration.

YUAN

During the Yuan dynasty many Sung-type wares continued to be made, especially Lung-ch'uan, Chun, and Ch'ing-pai. But new styles and techniques sprang up, the most notable of which was blue-and-white ware. This class of ceramic was made by painting with a cobalt pigment on a white body under a transparent glaze (Figure 3.18).

31

MING

With the beginning of the Ming dynasty in 1368, Chinese ceramics definitely entered a new era. From the classical, simple Sung ware, a change was made to lavish Victorian-type shapes, designs and colors. From this time until the present, one often has a problem in deciding whether the ceramics are gorgeous or garish (Figures 3.19 & 3.20). Among the impressive achievements of the Ming potter are fine, white bodies, and the common appearance of true porcelains. Also, a complete color palette was attained, although in many cases the colors were achieved by painting with low-fired enamels over the high-fired body glazes. Forming rose to new heights too, as did firing, so that almost any shape was made and fired, including some very large pieces.

Figure 3.19. A Ming blue-and-white dish.

Courtesy: The Smithsonian Institution, Freer Gallery of Art, Washington, D.C. (61.14)

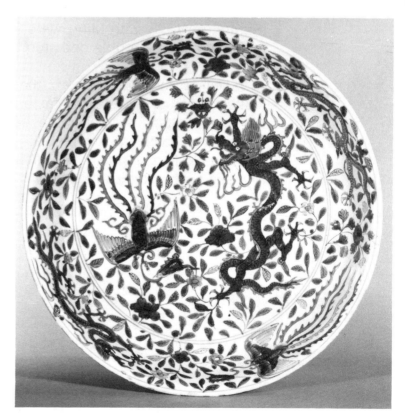

Figure 3.20. A Wan-li dish of the Ming dynasty.

Courtesy: The Metropolitan Museum of Art. Purchase: Rogers Fund, 1917. (17.118.17)

CH'ING

The Ch'ing dynasty ceramics, especially from Ching-te Chen, were remarkable for their size, colors, and intricate decoration (Figure 3.21). As with Ming ware, some very good pieces were made and some horrible ones too.

Inevitably the selection of Chinese ceramics comes down to a matter of personal taste. My taste happens to agree with that of the Sung potters, so that influenced my fabrication of pots and glazes. If my taste had happened to match Ch'ing or Ming, I would have had to find another field, because I wouldn't have been able to make such complex pieces and decorations.

Figure 3.21. A K'ang-hsi vase of the Ch'ing dynasty.

Purifying the Paste.

CHAPTER 4

YUEH WARE

Figure 4.1. Map of China showing Shang-lin Hu kiln site.

Yueh ceramics represent the beginning of consistant celadon glazes. And, as with the beginning of any new material or process, they are not as sophisticated as later types of the same species. Some of the early Yueh ceramics were made in southern Kiangsu and northern Chekiang provinces with much fine ware coming from Shang-lin Hu (Figure 4.1.) Its origin in time is from the Tang dynasty to early Sung.

Figure 4.2 Yueh bowl with incised phoenixes.

The export of Yueh ware was common, with sherds being found at excavation sites as far afield as Samarra on the Tigris, Fostat (Old Cairo), and Susa. Reasons for its popularity would be its grey-green glaze over a grey porcelaneous body, as well as the well-executed and artistic carving (Figure 4.2.)

Figure 4.3 Handsomely carved Yueh bowl.

The materials and techniques used were far in advance of pottery products to be found anywhere else in the world, and also, the artistry of such magnificent pieces as the dragon bowl in the Metropolitan Museum of Art were not surpassed anywhere (Figure 4.3.)

Figure 4.4. Lung-ch'uan celadon bowl.

Comparing Yueh ware with later, Lung-ch'uan celadons (Figure 4.4), one sees that the former is notable for its decorations, while the latter is a celadon that stands alone with its fat, unctuous glaze on simple unadorned bodies. Again and again we run into this circumstance in Chinese ceramics, with a glaze and body being perfectly mated with regard to color, thickness, decoration and shape.

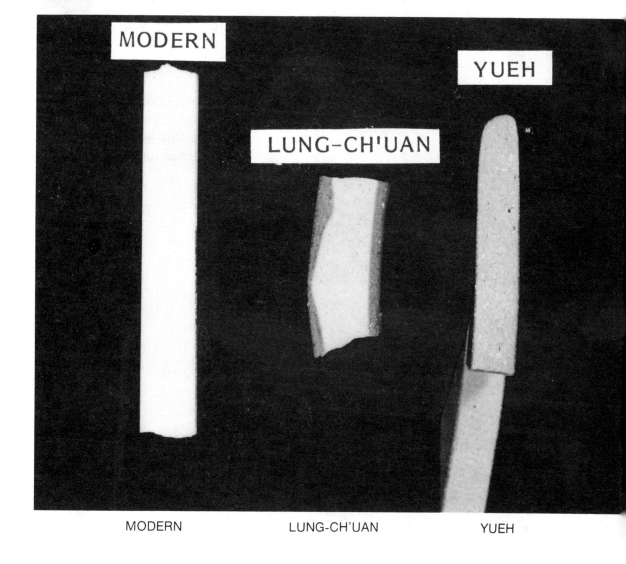

MODERN LUNG-CH'UAN YUEH

Figure 4.5. Comparison of body density and color.

There are, however, strong similarities between Yueh and Lung-ch'uan **bodies.** Both are fine-grained, dense and obviously high fired. The only difference between them and a modern, commercial chinaware is the fact that they both have a grey color (Figure 4.5).

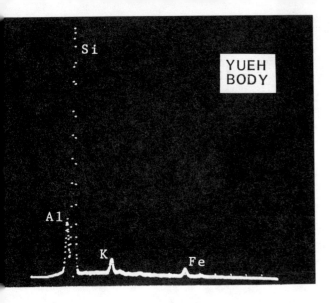

Figure 4.6. EDXR spectrum of Yueh body showing relatively high silica content compared to alumina and potash. This corroborates the SEM picture which shows many silica grains.

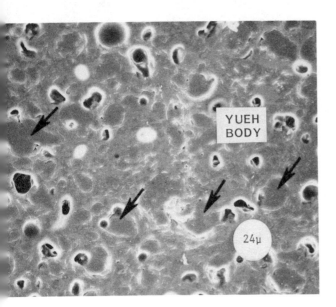

Figure 4.7. SEM of Yueh body showing many silica grains (500 x).

The composition of a typical Yueh body as determined by EDXR examination (Figure 4.6) is high in silica, and low in potash and alumina when compared to a Lung-ch'uan analysis. One deduces from this that it was easier to find siliceous raw materials near Shang-lin Hu than feldspathic ones.

A scanning electron micrograph of a Yueh body (Figure 4.7) illustrates many silica grains in the body, in agreement with the analytical results.

42

Figure 4.8. EDXR of Yueh glaze with high lime content and some magnesia. Otherwise the glaze composition is very similar to the body.

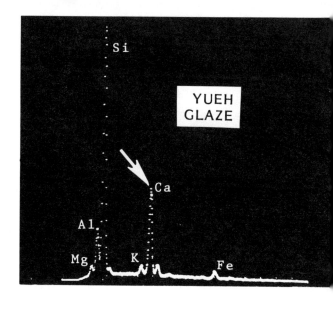

Figure 4.9. Optical micrograph of Yueh thin-section showing clear, thin glaze with bubbles at the glaze-body interface. (150 x).

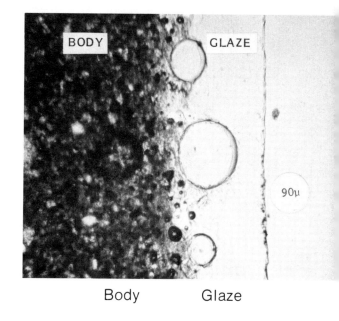

Body   Glaze

Yueh glazes have high lime contents (Figure 4.8) with low alumina and potash levels. One can very easily imagine a Yueh potter making a slurry of his body formulation, adding lime to it, grinding it to a fine slip and using it for a glaze. Since there is obviously a strong interaction between body and glaze (Figure 4.9) the glaze may not need to consist of much more than plain lime.

To make a Yueh type glaze, one could start with three parts of Cornwall Stone, one part of limestone (including dolomite) and a percent or less of iron oxide to give the pale green color. This glaze would be applied thinly and fired high in reduction to obtain a clear glaze over a light grey, dense body.

Actually there is not much reason to make a Yueh-type glaze, because its main importance is as a historic precursor to the thick, unctuous Sung celadons.

CHAPTER 5

LUNG-CH'UAN CELADONS

Figure 5.1. Map of Chekiang province.

Lung-ch'uan is the name of a mountain village situated in southern Chekiang province on a stream at the head-waters of the Ou-chiang (Figure 5.1). To appreciate the locale one should read the fascinating description by Palmgren of his 1936 search for sherds in Chekiang province (Sung Sherds-Palmgren, Sundius, & Steger-1963-Almqvist & Wiksell pp. 31-78).

The name Lung-ch'uan and the term "celadon" are almost synonymous because of the large number of classical celadon wares made at Lung-ch'uan locations during the Sung, Yuan, and Ming dynasties. Of importance also is the fact that a large quantity of this ware was exported, as evidenced by the sherds and complete pieces found in Japan, the Philippines, Samarra, and other sites.

This large export trade spread the fame of Chinese porcelain world-wide. It is particularly impressive that Chinese porcelain was regarded as a precious item wherever it appeared. Its hard glaze and body, resonant ring, simple shapes, and jade-like color had universal appeal since it could be immediately recognized as a unique item, superior in all ways to local pottery types.

The volume of Lung-ch'uan celadons must have been tremendous during the Sung dynasty. Evidence for this is found in the many large sherd heaps described by Palmgren (Loc. cit.) and Dr. Chen.[1] The large quantities, together with the uniform quality of the bodies implies that there were some large, high quality sources of clay for the Lung-ch'uan potters, and these plus an abundant fuel source must have been the determinants for the kiln sites.

Much of the Lung-ch'uan ware exhibits the soft, thick, green glaze usually regarded as the **TYPE** example for celadon (Figure 5.2). The book "Sung Sherds" by Palmgren, Sundius, and Steger gives a better view of Lung-ch'uan celadons, however, because it has excellent color plates showing all of the celadon color variations from near-blue through many kinds of green to brown. The selection process which occurred must have started right at the kiln sites, with the duller colors going out as peasant rice bowls, the medium quality ware going to the foreign market, and the finest being reserved for Chinese royalty.

1.) Toji, Vol. VII, No. 5, October, 1935.

Figure 5.2. A Kinuta celadon vase, whose soft, blue-green glaze resembles massed lard in texture.

The non-uniformity of celadon color must be kept in mind both when making celadon glazes and when viewing museum pieces. It is easy to think that all Lung-ch'uan celadons were a soft blue-green to green color, when actually a wide variation occurred in the kiln. Celadons are still touchy to make, for a slight variation in glaze thickness, firing temperature, or reducing conditions will result in a rather wide variation of color.

Lung-ch'uan celadon glazes can be almost blue when they are underfired and are compounded of materials low in titania and alumina. But, when such a glaze is fired progressively higher, it becomes greener in hue, grows more transparent, gets thinner, reacts with the body and generally shifts in color toward warmer tones. The softness of the glaze color is a direct function of the glaze thickness and its degree of underfiring. However, if a Lung-ch'uan type glaze is compounded with too much titania or iron, then yellow, brown, or muddy hues result, just as is the case when the fires are slightly oxidizing instead of slightly reducing.

If we are to make a Lung-ch'uan type celadon we must keep all necessary conditions as close to the original as possible. The key word here is '**necessary**'. For example, it is not **important** to fire with wood like the Chinese did, but it is **necessary** to fire under good reducing conditions.

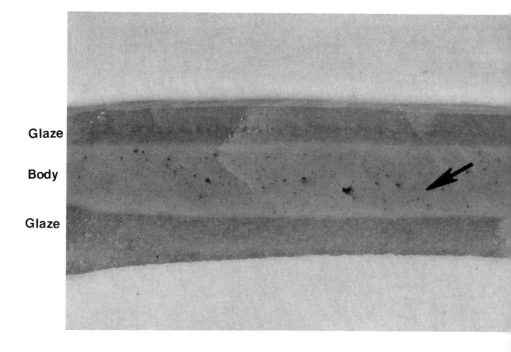

Glaze

Body

Glaze

Figure 5.3. Cross-section of a Lung-ch'uan body showing the dense structure and light grey color. (10 x)

Another **necessary** condition is the provision of a body with the appropriate texture and iron content (Figure 5.3). The body should be fine and smooth, yet it should contain 1-2% iron oxide. This can be accomplished by using a Georgia kaolin and a Kentucky ball clay plus enough extra iron oxide to give the desired degree of grey color. One should end up with the equivalent of a ''dirty'' porcelain body. The correct body color is essential to produce an appropriate celadon color, for too white a body produces a synthetic-looking green celadon.

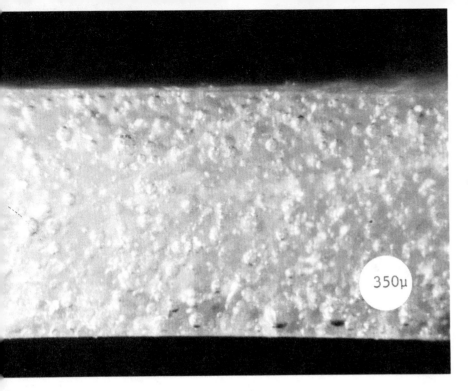

Glaze Surface

350μ

Figure 5.4. Close-up view of a Lung-ch'uan glaze surface illustrating the fine bubble structure and small undissolved crystals. (35 x)

The most important criteria for the final glaze color are the firing time and temperature. One should approach the final temperature very slowly and the glaze should remain decidedly on the underfired side. This produces a glaze which is full of fine bubbles and undissolved silica particles (Figure 5.4), resulting in an unctuous, mutton-fat type celadon. The slow approach ensures that a sugary surface does not result.

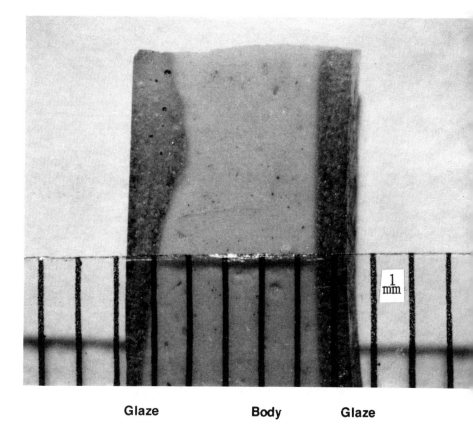

| Glaze | Body | Glaze |

Figure 5.5. Cross-section of a Lung-ch'uan ceramic comparing the glaze thickness with a millimeter scale (10 x).

Another critical requirement for a Sung-like celadon is a thick glaze. A 1-2 mm. thick glassy layer provides the feeling of depth that is part of the Lung-ch'uan celadon mystique (Figure 5.5). It is possible to obtain such thickness by one dip in a slurry, but a single or multiple spray coat may be needed in addition to avoid cracking and crawling. With a thick glaze such as this, underfiring becomes an absolute necessity in order to avoid glaze dripping and running. Much of the volume in the Lung-ch'uan sherd mountains is due to overfiring where pools of glaze have cemented sagger and ware into solid masses.

Using these factors of thick glazes and underfiring one can take any celadon glaze formulation, put it on a grey porcelain body, and make it look Sung-like. One of my favorite celadon recipes is the following:

> 51 parts Custer Feldspar
> 29 parts Supersil silica
> 11 parts Clay (your choice*)
> 20 parts Limestone
> 1 part Hematite or Magnetite

*English, Florida, or North Carolina kaolin will give bluer celadons; Georgia kaolin or Ball clay will give greener celadons.

The iron oxides should be very fine to avoid the appearance of spots, but in any case the glaze slip should be ball-milled about thirty minutes to disperse the iron. Firing will be very fussy. For example if one would normally fire this glaze to cone 8, then to achieve a Lung-ch'uan appearance it would be necessary to slowly fire to cone 6, hold for an hour and cool slowly. In any event glaze variations will probably occur as a function of kiln placement.

Since the Lung-ch'uan area of Chekiang province is the location of dozens of kiln sites (Figure 5.6), there is naturally no single type of ware that is representative of the whole area.

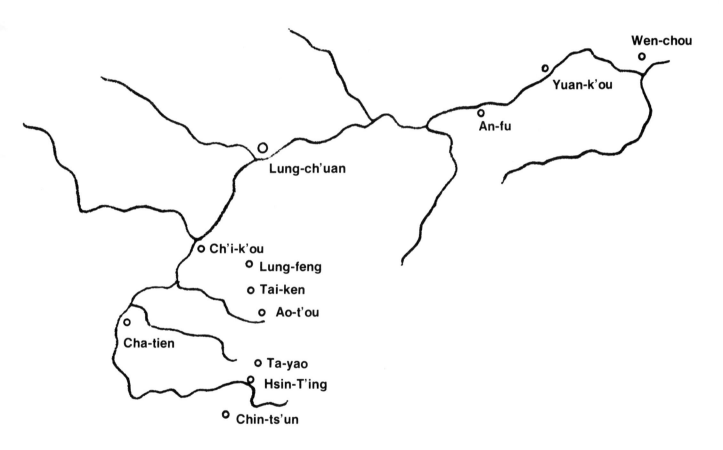

Figure 5.6. Kiln sites in the Lung-ch'uan region.

Still, there are certain characteristics of ceramics from the Lung-ch'uan region which are unique. We might say that:*

1. The bodies are dense though full of closed pores. (Fig. 5.3)

2. The bodies are light grey in color. (Fig. 5.3)

3. The bodies are fine textured and uniform. (Fig. 5.3)

4. The majority of bodies are thick (>2mm). (SS)

5. Glazes are predominantly blue-green to green. (SS)

6. Crackle is a 50-50 proposition. (SS)

7. Glazes tend to be thick (~1mm.). (Fig. 5.5)

8. Glazes are frequently layered. (SS)

9. Bubbly glazes are common. (Fig. 5.4)

10. Quartz relicts are common in glazes. (Fig. 5.7)

11. Glazes are modern in chemical type with moderate lime and alumina content. (Table I)

12. There is no wide variation in chemical composition among glazes or among bodies. (SS & Table I)

*Topics with the notation (SS) are well illustrated by the plates found in "Sung Sherds." Other notes refer to figures and tables in this chapter.

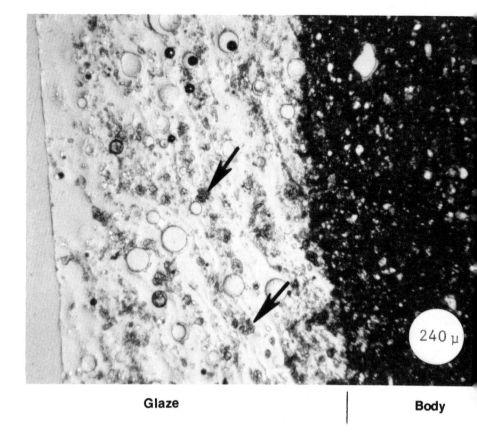

| Glaze | Body |

Figure 5.7. Optical micrograph of a Lung-ch'uan glaze and body in thin section (50 x), showing numerous bubbles and silica relicts (arrows) in the glaze.

Observation of Lung-ch'uan glazes by both optical and scanning electron microscopes has been very useful in detecting the original composition and firing conditions. Figure 5.7, an optical view of a thin section, clearly shows the quartz relicts and gas bubbles in a Lung-ch'uan glaze. Both of these conditions indicate that the glaze was not fired to maturity. In addition, the quartz relicts are evidence that fine sand was used as a glaze raw material.

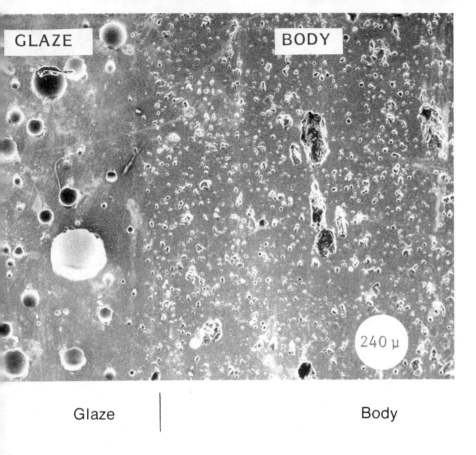

GLAZE   BODY

240 μ

Glaze | Body

**Figure 5.8. SEM of a Lung-ch'uan
body and glaze illustrating
the fine, closed pores in the
body and bubbles in the
glaze. (50 x).**

All the physical evidence on Lung-ch'uan ware points to a good clay raw material and an abundant feldspar source. The ware has been fired higher than Kuan since the body is dense, but not as high as Chun and Northern Celadon, because there are many fine bubbles and undissolved quartz grains found in the glazes.

Figure 5.8, a scanning electron micrograph, illustrates the glaze bubbles more graphically than Figure 5.7. The small body pores in Figure 5.8 are evidence of a fine body texture that may be due either to a high quality clay source, or to extensive working of the body.

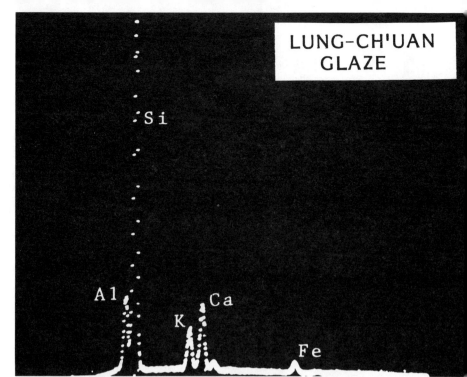

Figure 5.9. EDXR spectrum of a Lung-ch'uan glaze.

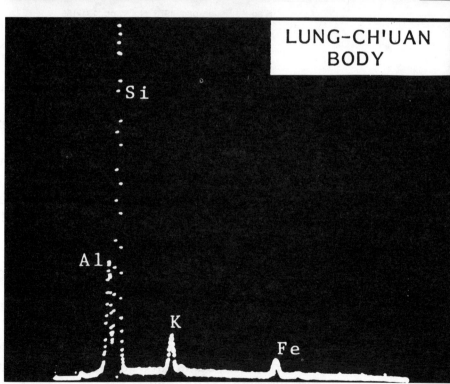

Figure 5.10. EDXR spectrum of a Lung-ch'uan body.

Analysis by energy dispersive X-ray technique in the scanning electron microscope (Figures 5.9 & 5.10) gives a qualitative analysis that compares well with other Lung-ch'uan samples (Table I) analyzed by Sundius and reported in a recent Chinese analysis.

TABLE I
Analyses of Lung-ch'uan Sung Sherds

	Chinese[2] Glaze Analysis	Sundius[3] Glaze Analysis	Chinese[2] Body Analysis	Sundius[3] Body Analysis
SiO_2	69.16	68.59	67.82	67.43
Al_2O_3	15.40	14.28	23.93	24.48
CaO	8.39	10.40	——	0.12
MgO	0.64	0.40	0.26	0.30
K_2O	4.87	4.97	5.32	4.52
Na_2O	0.32	0.14	0.32	0.40
TiO_2	——	0.02	0.22	0.18
Fe_2O_3	0.95	0.73	2.10	2.38
MnO_2	——	n.d.	0.03	0.02

[2]K'ao-ku Hsueh-pao, 1973, No. 1, pp. 131-156.
[3]Sung Sherds — Palmgren, N., Steger, W., and Sundius, N. (1963) Stockholm. Page 439.

These glaze analyses immediately remind one of a low-potash feldspar composition with added lime. On the other hand the bodies must have been more complicated. They could have been formulated with equal parts of high potash feldspar and kaolin plus added silica. At least that is how we would do the same thing today. Since their raw materials contained breakdown products of granitic rocks, there may have been natural formations near Lung-ch'uan that required only the addition of clay to make this body formula.

Summarizing, an ideal Lung-ch'uan celadon has a thick, unctuous, blue-green to green glaze over a grey porcelaneous body.

Such a glaze can be a simple lime-feldspar-flint-clay-iron composition, but is strongly dependent on auxiliary conditions for its ultimate exotic look.

The glaze should be thickly applied.

It should be definitely underfired (in reduction).

And it should be applied over an iron-grey body.

CHAPTER 6

TING AND TZU-CHOU WARE

Courtesy: The Smithsonian Institution, Freer Gallery of Art, Washington, D.C. (63.16)

Figure 6.1. Ting Plate

There needs to be a note here on why Ting and Tzu-chou ware are not discussed in detail in this book. The best reason would seem to be that they are not celadons, but that excuse is not valid because Chien ware is covered.

TING WARE

Frankly, Ting ware (Figure 6.1.) does not appeal to me! I have always had a dislike for ivory and cream colors and have never intentionally made a ceramic piece with such a glaze.

Nevertheless, Ting ceramics are related to the Sung celadons, certainly in design, and probably in glaze type. The carved and molded Ting designs are definitely remindful of Northern celadon pieces even though there is no close resemblance of exact patterns. It is as if the same artisans were doing the carving, but different designers were making up the patterns.

With the glazes, there are certain cream-to-yellow hues that will remind the maker of celadons of occasions when a kiln has gone oxidizing. Other, ivory colors are probably just examples of highly purified glazes. The complete lack of bluish or greenish hues in Ting ware is striking, and points to masterful control of kiln atmospheres and a total change from the usual reducing atmosphere found in other Sung kilns.

TZ'U-CHOU WARE

Tz'u-chou ware is appealing because of its bold designs, striking forms, and massive sizes. These potters used slips, glazes, carving, and sgraffito techniques to decorate their ware, with a freedom in decoration which makes them outstanding. A close examination of their designs quickly reveals that they were executed in a forthright manner. There is no evidence of a cramped style or any attempts at corrections of mistakes. There is just a free-flowing painting or carving. Up close they may look a little sloppy, but from ten feet away they are magnificent.

From a historic point of view, there is a feeling that the Tz'u-chou potters were preparing the way for Ching-te Chen and the Ming potters. If one looks at a vase from Tz'u-chou (Figure 6.4) and then at a Ming vase from Ching-te Chen (Figure 6.3), the feeling of déja-vu is overpowering. Tz'u-chou ware is certainly more varied in size, color and design than any other Sung ceramic.

Figure 6.3. Porcelain vase, Ming dynasty.

Courtesy: The Metropolitan Museum of Art. Bequest of J.D. Rockefeller, Jr., 1960. (1961.200.52)

Figure 6.4. Tz'u Chou vase, Sung dynasty.

Although I should know better than to suggest this, I will anyway. Tz'u-chou should be easy to duplicate! It probably isn't, but one would expect that a white slip and an overcoat of an iron-brown glaze would work in one instance (Figure 6.2). And in another case (Figure 6.4) an iron-brown base glaze decorated with a higher iron-content slip would be the way to start.

I was once naive enough to believe statements like this about ceramics. Now I know better, and hopefully the readers of this book will too, since there is nothing "easy" in the realm of ceramics.

CHAPTER 7

CHUN WARE

Courtesy: The Metropolitan Museum of Art. Bequest of Mary Stillman Harkness, 1950. (50.145.316)

Figure 7.1. Blue Chun bubble bowl with purple splash.

Chun ware is another uniquely glazed Chinese ceramic. Its pale-to-deep blue color with an occasional splash of copper red presents a bright appearance which is appealing to current tastes (Figure 7.1). It probably was not so popular among the other, sober glazes of the Sung dynasty.

Figure 7.2. Chun flower pot of a period later than Sung.

Incidentally, this description and discussion of Chun ware will be limited to the more subdued early Chun types of North China. The later Chun with its flambuoyant streaked, red-blue-purple, blotchy glazes on flower pots (Figure 7.2) and bulb holders will not be considered here.

Figure 7.3. Pale Chun vase.

The bowls, vases, and plates in Chun ware vary in color from pale blue (Figure 7.3) to a bright blue color. This blue is always on the green side of the spectrum however, and never on the purple-red edge (like cobalt colored glazes).

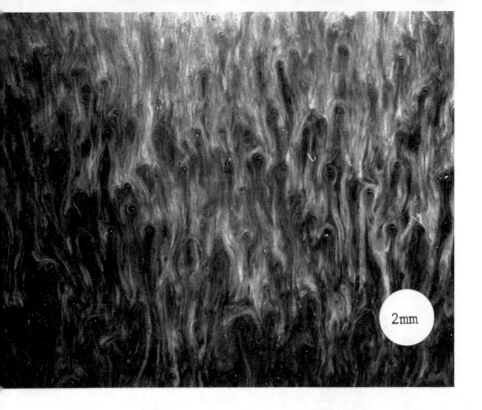

Figure 7.4. Hare's-fur pattern formed by runny glaze on Chun reproduction. (6x).

Another distinctive feature of Chun other than the blue color is the frequent occurrence of vertical streaks in the glaze (Figure 7.4). This is often referred to as a hare's-fur pattern, as in the brown Chien glaze.

There is another characteristic of Chun ware that is unique for Sung glazes and that is its opalescence. While other Sung glazes such as Kuan and Lung-ch'uan are phase-separated and soft in color due to bubbles and fine crystals, Chun is a true opal with a brown color in transmitted light and a blue color in reflected light. (Sung Sherds-Sundius- pages 408-413).

Chun was my first introduction to the mystery of Sung glazes thanks to a sample sherd from Margaret Medley. The search was on then to find out why an iron celadon was sometimes blue and sometimes green. The hunt lead through hundreds of syntheses and analyses, but finally came to a twisting, stumbling, lurching conclusion.

It happened in the following way:

The first step came about through synthesis. By working backwards from complex green celadons to the simplest glaze conceivable, it was found that green celadons were formed from trace materials in normal glaze batches. If one went to a simple batch containing just lime and feldspar, then blue celadons were not only possible, but were common. The secret ingredient was **Titanium**, a common trace material in clays that forms green colors in the presence of reduced iron.

The next step was to emphasize the blue color by opalization, and again synthesis showed the way. It was known from glass-making experience that opals could be formed in many ways, so these were all tested to find the most probable system that could have been used by the Sung Chinese.

A starting glaze was chosen that was close in composition to analysed Chun and then opalizing agents were added. Fluoride worked, but it never had been reported in Chinese glazes. High lime contents also formed opals, but they were far outside the analysis range. Finally, Phosphate seemed to be just right. In low concentrations it formed a dense opal that emphasized the blue in Chun-like glazes.

The phosphate result was rather puzzling, however, because 5-10% phosphate is required to opalize an ordinary glass (1.) and only 0.5% phosphate was required for this Chun glaze. Finally after more syntheses, it was found that Chun is really a high silica opal that is triggered and accentuated by phosphate. A lovely blue opal can be formed by adding more and more silica to a lime-feldspar glaze, but at any stage of the process the opal can be greatly intensified by the addition of 0.5% phosphate.

----

(1) "Industrial Ceramics" — Singer & Singer — p. 588 ref. S212. The lowest percentage of P_2O_5 found is 7.84%.

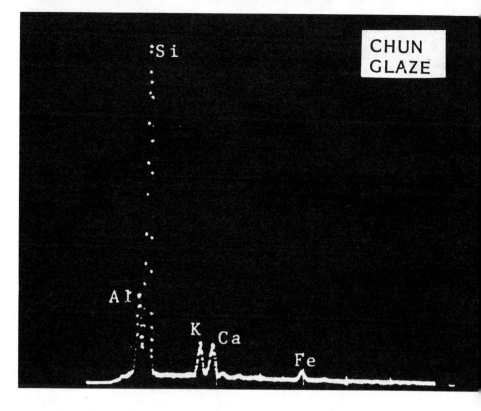

Figure 7.5. EDXR spectrum of a Chun glaze.

An EDXR spectrum of a Chun sherd demonstrates the high silica content of the glaze (Figure 7.5). The phosphate level is too low to be identified by this analytical technique.

The Chinese undoubtedly provided the phosphate by ash additions to the glaze slip. Many ashes contain 5% phosphate, thus a 10% ash addition to a glaze would provide 0.5% phosphate. I have used a 1% bone ash supplement to get the same effect and yet avoid other complicating contaminants. Since ash was the component giving hare's-fur effects in Chien glazes, it would be performing the same duty in Chun.

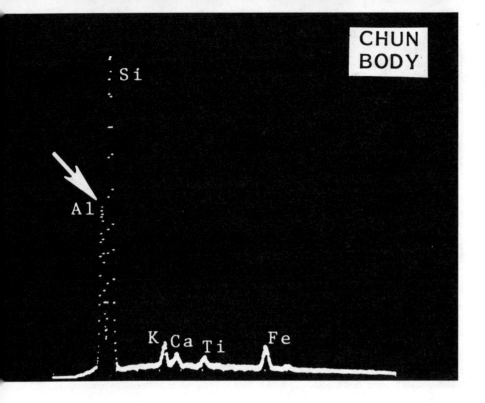

Figure 7.6. EDXR spectrum of a Chun body showing high alumina content.

The bodies of some early Chun ware are a little unusual for Sung because they are rather porous and sandy appearing in contrast to the porcelaneous nature of other contemporary bodies (Lung-ch'uan, Yueh, Ting). It almost appears to be underfired, but this cannot be true, because the high silica Chun glaze must be high fired. What it amounts to is that the Chun body is quite refractory and lacking in fluxes, therefore even though it is high fired, it has not become dense. Figure 7.6 is an energy-dispersive x-ray diagram of a Chun body analysis and it shows the high alumina, low potash content which would make this Chun body quite refractory.

Figure 7.7a. A contemporary Chun bowl, inside view. Copper nitrate solution was spotted on the inside surface of the bisque. After glaze firing the copper diffused through the glaze on the inside surface.

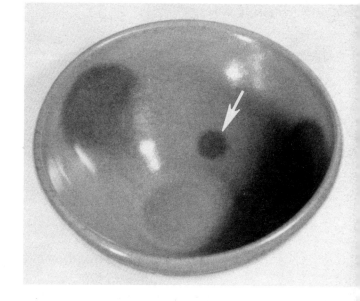

Figure 7.7b. An outside view of the bowl in Figure 7.7a. Copper has diffused through the bowl in the same pattern as above and formed red spots on the outside glaze.

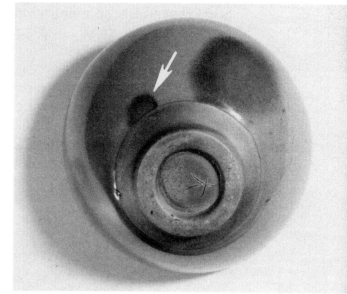

The red-to-purple splashes on Chun pieces are about as intriguing and complex as the glaze itself. Fundamentally these markings are due to copper-rich areas. An analysis of their origin is complicated by the fact that copper is both mobile and fugitive in high temperature, reducing fires.

Copper's mobility can be demonstrated by painting the inside surface of a bisqued bowl with copper nitrate solution (Figures 7.7a & 7.7b). After glazing and reduction firing, the copper-red color will be found on the **outside** glaze surface. Its fugitive nature can be discovered by comparing both fast firing and extended firing on similar pieces, in which case the copper is found to have volatilized from the long-fired piece.

There are a number of choices available if one wants to apply copper to ware. One can make solutions of copper nitrate or sulfate and paint these either on the body or on the raw glaze. However, the concentration of the solution is critical, for with too little copper there is no color at all, and with too much copper, greens result.

Insoluble copper compounds can also be applied. And again the concentrations are important. Copper carbonate is easier to apply than copper oxide, but either compound trends to a dark green color when applications are heavy. It is comforting to know that the Chinese had the same problems, for their copper splashes are often either faint or discolored by green patches.

There is one more cautionary point on Chun glazes. This is in regard to the bubbling on the glaze surface. Many glazes have myriads of fine bubbles trapped in them, but few have the trouble that Chun does with these bubbles being enlarged and broken on the surface (Figure 7.8). This is a problem that the Sung potters had and that you may have too. The causes are twofold:

1. The glaze is viscous and high-fired.

2. There is phosphate present in a high temperature reduction firing.

Because the glaze is so viscous, the bubbles are retained for longer times than normal. And because the temperatures are extra high, the cooling rate is more rapid than usual.

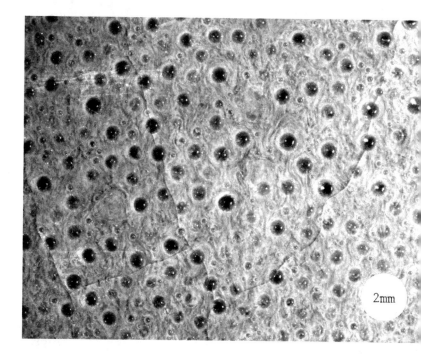

2mm

Figure 7.8. Large bubbles, caused by phosphate decomposition in a Chun reproduction. (6 x).

Phosphates are the **major** cause of large bubbles in Chun ware though. Without phosphate there is no problem (and of course, no Chun). There seems to be either a thermal decomposition of phosphate, or a chemical reduction of phosphate occurring. One possible solution is a short hold at maximum kiln temperature using an oxidizing atmosphere. Another solution is a gradual cooling from maximum temperature in order to allow the bubbles to break and/or redissolve. It is hard to evaluate the results of these treatments because the bubbly condition does not always occur, even without counteractions.

Since opal formation depends on low alumina content of the glaze, Cornwall stone is a good base material because of its high silica content. Of course the same result can be obtained by using feldspars with added silica. One of my recipes consists of:

48 parts	Potash Feldspar
31 parts	Silica
20 parts	Limestone
1 part	Bone Ash
1 part	Magnetite

The Sung potters probably used a crushed granite-like material, high in silica and contaminated with the correct quantity of iron, plus a wood ash to furnish lime, phosphate, and potash.

Since the fugacity of copper will depend on your personal style of firing, you must experiment with the copper splash material. A logical test would be to mix 1,3, & 10% copper carbonate with dollops of glaze, and brush patches of these on the raw glaze before firing. One should not be discouraged by problems with copper red, since the Sung potters never were successful in solving this situation either.

A chemical analysis of a violet Chun glaze was reported in "Sung Sherds" by Sundius (page 416).

SiO_2	— 72.79%
Al_2O_3	— 9.94
Fe_2O_3	— 1.58
TiO_2	— 0.07
MgO	— 1.50
CaO	— 8.80
Na_2O	— 0.72
K_2O	— 3.85
P_2O_5	— 0.54

All of the requirements for a Chun opal can be noted here, the moderate alumina and high silica content and the presence of phosphate. And in addition, the necessary conditions for blue coloration are present, namely a moderate iron level and a very low titania content.

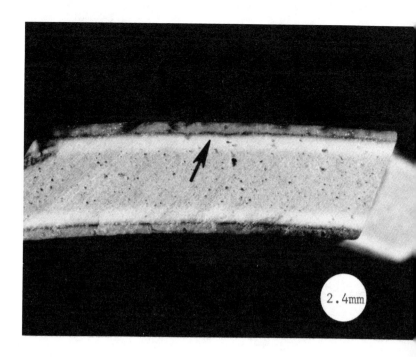

Figure 7.9. Cross-section of Chun sherd showing bleach layer in body below glaze. (5 x).

Microscopy of Chun sherds was very informative. As mentioned, the opalescence was quite striking. For example, on a thin section the blue color was very evident with incident light, but with transmitted light the same piece was a decided amber.

At low magnification (Figure 7.9) a marked bleach layer can be seen in the body just under the glaze.

40μ

Figure 7.10a & b. Crystalline reaction zone between Chun glaze and body. (315 x & 1050 x).

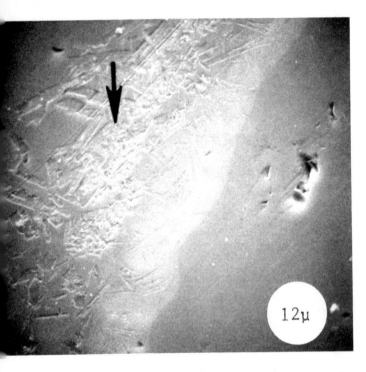

12μ

At higher magnification a sharp crystal layer is visible between the glaze and body (Figure 7.10a) and at still higher magnification this crystal layer is shown to be quite complex (Figure 7.10b).

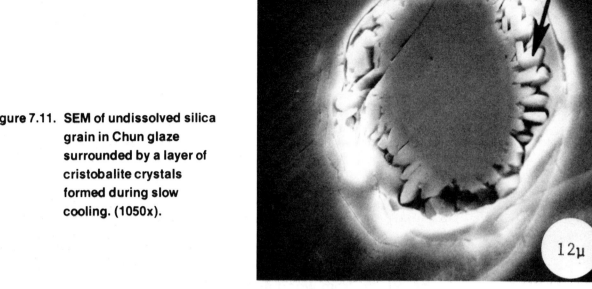

Figure 7.11. SEM of undissolved silica grain in Chun glaze surrounded by a layer of cristobalite crystals formed during slow cooling. (1050x).

12µ

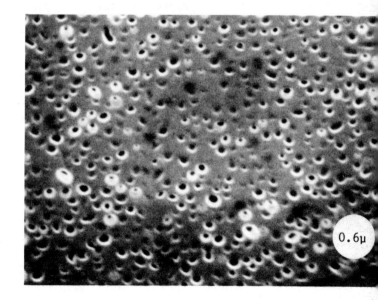

Figure 7.12. SEM of phase-separated droplets in opal region of Chun glaze. (20,000x).

0.6µ

Another high magnification view of the glaze (Figure 7.11) illustrates undissolved silica stones with thick surrounding layers of cristobalite. At very high magnification (Figure 7.12) droplets of a second glass phase can be seen in regions where opalization is observed visually.

An interpretation of these microscopic features is:

1. The bleach layer is due to a soluble glaze component that has diffused into the body, possibly potassium carbonate from wood ash.

2. The crystalline interlayer is due to interaction between the glaze fluxes and the body. The large size of the crystals is due to the high firing and very slow cooling.

3. The undissolved silica stones in the glaze show that large sized sand was used in the batch, while the surrounding cristobalite crystals indicate again that slow cooling occurred.

4. The small glass droplets in the glaze represent the separated glass phase that is responsible for opalization. These also reflect a slow cooling process.

In summary, we have seen that Chun ware is a high fired blue celadon with a coarse refractory body. The blue glaze is due to reduced iron in a siliceous base glaze to which added phosphate gives a marked opalescence. The occasional red-to-purple accents on the glaze are due to splashes of copper applied over or under the glaze layer. While the Sung Chun glaze was probably made with wood ash and a granitic stone, our replicas can be formed from a feldspar and silica mix with lime and bone ash added.

CHAPTER 8

NORTHERN CELADONS

Courtesy of the Fitzwilliam Museum, Cambridge.

Figure 8.1. A Northern Celadon dish with an olive-green glaze over a freely carved design.

There is a class of Sung ceramics known as Northern celadon which consists of an olive-green to grey-green glaze, thinly laid over deeply carved or molded bodies (Figure 8.1.). This is one Sung glaze that is not thick and unctuous and enigmatic, in fact the only question about Northern celadons is whether the peculiar khaki colors originated from glaze constituents or from firing conditions.

The mystique of Northern celadons is primarily due to the intricate and artistic designs carved or molded into their surface. One immediately suspects that these ceramics are fairly close relatives of Yueh ware, just developed at a later time in another place. Certainly this glaze, like Yueh, is not unique enough to stand alone as a beautiful glaze without the spendid designs accompanying it.

The mechanics and chemistry of Northern celadon glazes seem to come about like this: The glaze is high in lime content, as shown by EDXR (Figure 8.2.), and has been fired to high temperatures (cone 8-12). The latter conclusion is deduced from the clarity of cross-sections, showing clear bubble-free glazes, strongly reacted with the body (Figure 8.3.). In this optical micrograph one can see the body dissolving, with pieces floating off into the glaze.

The reaction of the glaze with the body has been found by experiment to be very important to the final glaze color. A wide range of hues, from a clear green to a deep brown can be obtained merely by varying the time and temperature of firing as well as the impurity level in the body. It has been suggested by others that the variation in celadon colors from green to brown is due solely to changing oxidation conditions in the kiln. This is certainly a factor, but experimental verification of the importance of chemical contaminants means that the atmospheric conditions should be assigned only a minor role. Figure 8.3 illustrates the strong reaction between glaze and body in a Northern celadon sherd.

The colors obtained are derived from various combinations of iron and titanium. Iron levels are obtained both from intentionally added iron colorants and from impurities in the glaze and body raw materials. Titanium content of the glaze is due solely to impurities, a small amount deriving from the glaze batch (normally giving the celadon green color) but most coming from the body when the coloration has advanced into the brown region.

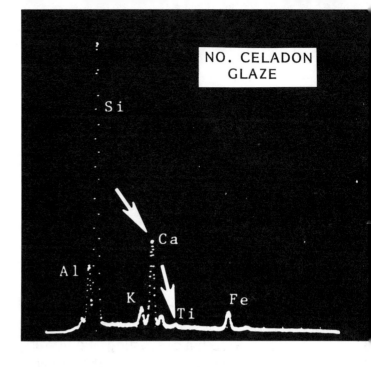

Figure 8.2. EDXR spectrum of a
Northern Celadon glaze
showing the high lime
content which at high
temperatures would react
strongly with the body.

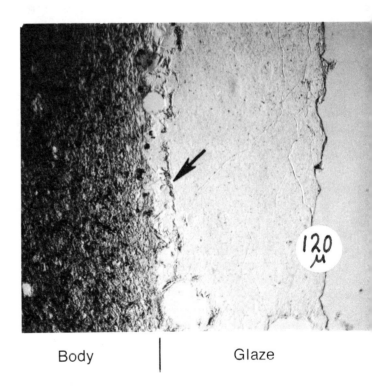

Figure 8.3. Optical micrograph of a
Northern Celadon glaze
cross-section (100x)
showing it to be clear and
to have reacted strongly
with the body.

81

Coloration from iron alone is not simple, because the color does not just intensify with increasing iron content. One finds that both a deepening of color and a shifting of color occurs. The shift from a relatively pure blue or blue-green at low concentrations to deeper and muddier colors at high concentrations is due in part to shifting ratios of ferric oxide and ferrous oxide.*

The color of the two iron oxides is not just a simple additive blending of two hues either. We are faced with the possibility of colors due to ferrous oxide, ferric oxide and mixed oxides as well as ferrites in the rather alkaline glazes.

In case this complicated iron situation were not bad enough, titanium enters into the picture by forming strongly colored titanium-iron complexes. Evidently a little bit of titanium goes a long way in producing brown colors with iron in glazes.

---

*This change in the ferrous-ferric oxide ratio can be independent of the atmospheric redox conditions. This is due to the termal decomposition of ferric oxide at elevated temperatures. Even in an air atmosphere, the reaction:

$$Fe_2O_3 \longrightarrow 2\ FeO\ +\ 1/2\ O_2$$

will proceed to the right when the partial pressure of the evolving oxygen exceeds 1/5 of an atmosphere.

This latter case can be evaluated experimentally by firing celadon glazes on dirty bodies. If one uses fast firing, blues-to-greens can be obtained. But, by extending the time and temperature of firing, these same glazes and bodies will produce yellower and muddier colors until finally really brown glazes result.

This effect is most noticeable on Northern celadon pieces because the glazes are:

1. Thin, hence they react completely with the body;

2. They are clear, hence there is no opacity to hide the color;

3. They are high in lime, thus they are more apt to react with the body;

4. They are high fired, which also encourages glaze-body reaction.

The net effect is to make it difficult to obtain one specific color when preparing Northern celadon replicas. What should be a straight forward glaze is made complicated by body contamination with very effective coloring agents (i.e. Ti & Fe).

Figure 8.4. Northern Celadon-type bowl with molded design under olive glaze. (Replica)

An interesting sidelight to Northern celadons is the need for a subdued color over the complex carvings. If one covers such a decorated body with a brightly colored glaze or even an elegant glaze like Kuan, it just doesn't match. A bright glaze detracts from the carving, and the carving detracts from the glaze. The point of this argument is: while one can criticize the olive-colored Northern celadon pieces, an analysis soon shows that this is the perfect color for such decorated ware (Figure 8.4).

To fabricate a Northern celadon colored glaze one only has to start with a normal celadon glaze batch, and add to it an additional percent of iron oxide, and about five percent additional limestone. From there on it is up to the body and the firing technique to finish the job. The body should contain 1-2% iron oxide and as close to 1% titanium dioxide as possible. A long, strong firing will then allow a thin glaze layer to pick up the necessary impurities for an olive colored celadon. If the attack is too strong one should back off on the lime and ease up on the firing conditions. Naturally the firing should be in reduction.

CHAPTER 9

SOUTHERN SUNG KUAN WARE

Kuan (Imperial) ware was made at least as early as the Northern Sung era, but identification of pieces as definite: **Northern** types is rather hazy. On the other hand identification of Southern Sung Kuan is on a better footing, because a kiln site was found near Hangchow with typical Kuan sherds and some sagger material.(1).

There is a wide variety of coloration in Kuan pieces as can be seen in illustrations of Porcelain of the National Palace Museum (2). There are cream colors, pale blues and greens, and near-white. But the glazes are always thick, crackled, and opaque. Similarly, the bodies are dark-colored and thin.

---

(1). A Handbook of Chinese Ceramics — Valenstein S.G. — Metropolitan Museum of Art — 1975 — p. 84.

(2). Kuan Ware of the Southern Sung Dynasty — Book 1 (part 2) — Cafa — Hongkong — 1962.

Figure 9.1. Kuan dish.

Even with many possible variations, there is what one would call a classical Southern Kuan piece, just as one could pick out a classical Lung-ch'uan or Chun ceramic. Such Kuan ware could be typified by the fabulous plate located in the Metropolitan Museum of Art (Figure 9.1) or by the priceless Kuan vase in the Percival David collection (Figure 9.2).

Figure 9.2. Kuan vase.

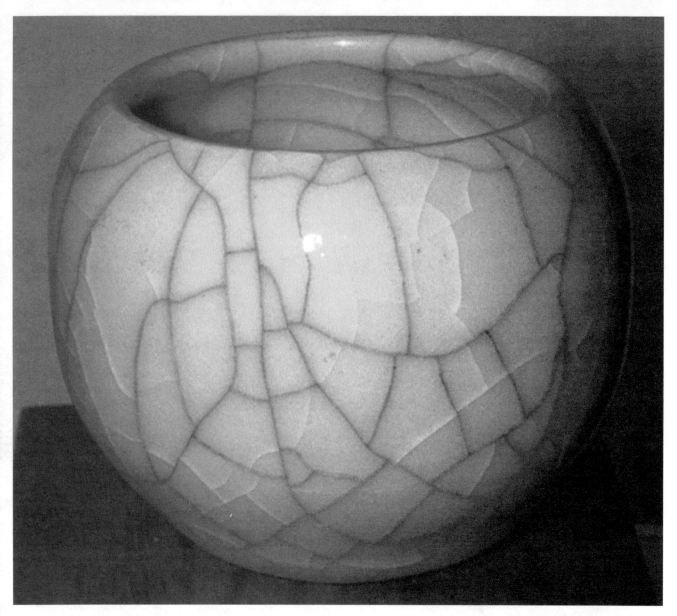

Figure 9.3. Replica of a Kuan bowl.

Kuan ware is the most beautiful of all Sung ceramics to me. With its soft, subtle colors, simple shapes and large random crackle, it is most appealing. It is also one of the simplest Sung glazes to duplicate as can be noted in the replica illustrated in Figure 9.3.

Glaze

Body

200μ

Figure 9.4. Crack in Kuan glaze penetrating the body, but terminating among the body grains. (60x)

An important characteristic of Kuan ware which sets it apart from its contemporaries, is its dark, though finely textured body. It is not really a black porcelain, because the ware has not been fired high enough to vitrify the body. This relatively low firing (perhaps cone 5) probably enables Kuan ware to exhibit fair strength because of the phenomenon of micro-cracking.

Phenomenologically, what we see in cross-section is this: The glaze cracks actually continue into the body (Figure 9.4). If this body were vitreous, then the crack would propagate through the piece and cause failure. With a softer, microcracked body, the large cracks can be dissipated in several directions without leading to immediate failure. Naturally this situation will not have the strength of a vitreous body and un-cracked glaze, but at least it will survive.

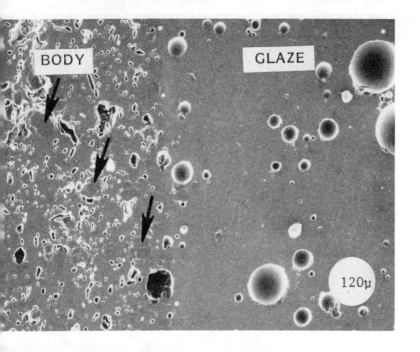

Figure 9.5a. SEM of Kuan body illustrating porosity and many silica grains (arrows). (100 x)

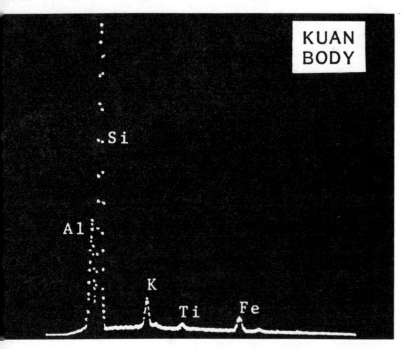

Figure 9.5b. EDXR spectrum of Kuan body, illustrating relatively high silica content.

Southern Sung Kuan bodies, as noted, are dark in color, but in addition, they are quite granular due to the presence of a high percentage of fine sand. This sand acts as a grog in the body.

Figure 9.5a is a Scanning Electron Micrograph of a Kuan body at low magnification showing the numerous silica grains and a high porosity. Figure 9.5b is an EDXR spectrum of the whole body illustrating a typical Sung composition with a moderate amount of iron present.

Figure 9.6a. Kuan bowl with brown mouth.

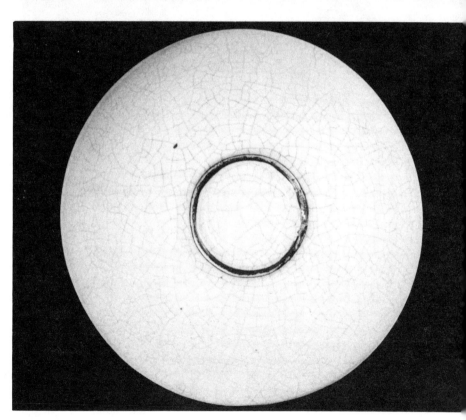

Figure 9.6b. Kuan bowl showing "iron foot".

The dark body is essential to obtain the feeling of depth in the glaze as well as to get the "brown mouth" and "iron foot" characteristic of Kuan (Figure 9.6a & b). My procedure has been to add 10% of Barnard slip clay to a porcelain body in order to get the desired degree of darkening.

The Chinese frequently used a dark slip on the foot to exaggerate the effect.

Figure 9.7. Cross-section of Kuan sherd comparing thickness of glaze and body to the thickness of a dime.

A remarkable feature of Kuan ware is the extreme thin-ness of the body in conjunction with a thick glaze (Figure 9.7). The Chinese undoubtedly threw the ware on a potter's wheel and then pared it down to a 1-2 mm. thickness. Probably if one concentrated on doing this for a life's work, one could get quite good at it, but for us mere humans, trying to make a few dozen pieces, it is recommended that slip-casting be tried. And even with cast pieces the problems are not small! Warpage during firing is a serious problem, and applying a thick glaze is a formidable task.

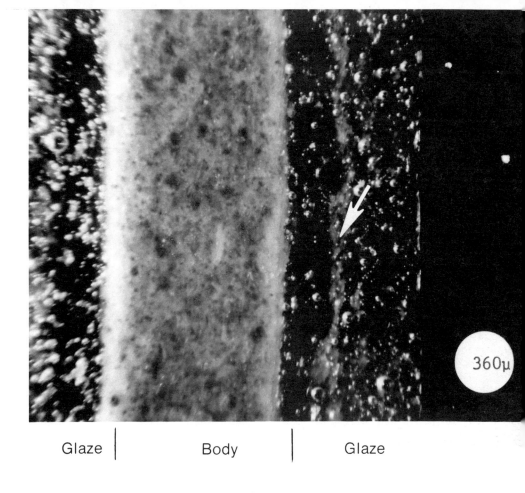

| Glaze | Body | Glaze |

360μ

Figure 9.8. Cross-section of Kuan body and glaze showing layering of the glaze and relative thickness of the glaze and body. (35 x)

On thick bodies one can dip coat about twice without peeling problems, but with thin bodies this won't work. A single dip coat can be made, then spraying must be resorted to. Cross-sections of Sung Kuan sherds (Figure 9.8) reveal about four coats were used by the Chinese. Since it is possible to get the Kuan glaze effect on thick bodies, the process of obtaining thinner and thinner bodies can be approached gradually. The glaze does need to be thick, however, to realize the translucent depth effect of Kuan ware.

Figure 9.9a. Picture of a Kuan glaze duplication with high lime content, slightly underfired. The crackle pattern was darkened with India ink.

Figure 9.9b. Same glaze and body as in Figure 9.9a. but fired to maturity. Note clearer glaze, no crackle, and drip at base due to glaze flow.

The importance of firing temperature on Kuan-type glazes can be seen in figures 9.9a & b. This is the sort of difference that is noted between Kuan and Northern Celadon glazes.

Figure 9.10. Overview of Kuan bowl.

The crackle on Kuan ware is ubiquitous. Whereas other Sung ceramics, like Lung-ch'uan, are sometimes crackled and sometimes not, Kuan is 100% crackled. This is because the glaze is underfired. It has to be underfired because of its great thickness. If it were even slightly over-fired, the glaze would run off the body, and there is no evidence of much glaze flow on Kuan pieces (Figure 9.10).

Figure 9.11. Kuan sherd showing fine bubble structure and crackle (2 x).

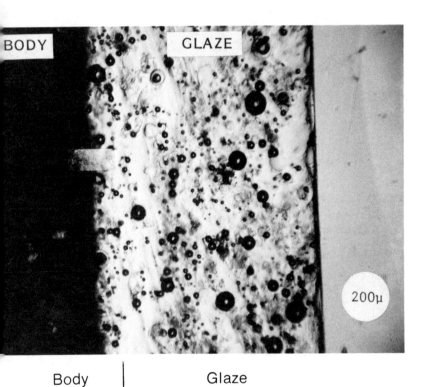

Body | Glaze

Figure 9.12. Kuan glaze layer in transmitted light showing bubbles and undissolved batch material. (60 x)

The Kuan sherd in Figure 9.11., and the thin section of the same piece in Figure 9.12, illustrate the effect of underfiring with the presence of many bubbles and much unmelted raw material.

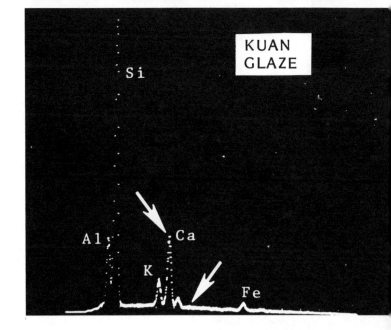

Figure 9.13a. EDXR spectrum of Kuan glaze showing high lime content and low titania level.

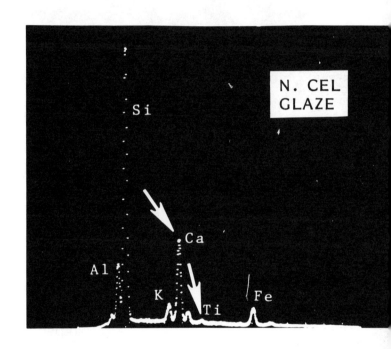

Figure 9.13b. EDXR spectrum of Northern celadon glaze.

Analytically, Kuan glazes are not vastly different in compositon from such glazes as Northern Celadons. The EDXR spectrum in Figure 9.13a shows that the glaze is only lower in iron and titania than the Northern Celadon analysis in Figure 9.13b. It, too, is remarkable for its high lime content. The difference in appearance between Kuan and Northern Celadons is due to the fact that the former is a thick glaze that has been underfired and the latter is a thin, over-fired glaze.

Figure 9.14. Kuan ware replica.

A Kuan glaze can start out as simply as:

> 80 parts Feldspar
> 20 parts Limestone
> 1 part Iron Oxide

The feldspar may be blended with Cornwall stone or silica to obtain the right expansion so that the desired crackle pattern is generated (Figure 9.14). The higher feldspar levels give finer crackle patterns. The lime content may also be raised to adjust the crackle and to promote a matte finish. A slight amount of phosphate (0.5% bone ash finely ground) also encourages a slight opalization.

98

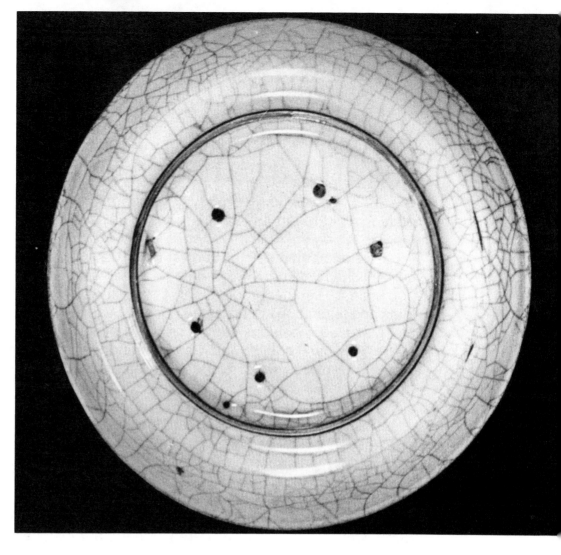

Figure 9.15. The base of a Kuan piece showing spur marks and bare patches of dark body.

It may be necessary to wipe some glaze off the rim of a piece to obtain a brown mouth, but there is usually just enough flow to provide this effect. Some Kuan pieces have glazed feet (Figure 9.15) and they have been fired on stilts. Others have just the bottom rim wiped off (Figure 9.6b).

To stain the crackle lines I resort to India ink for black lines and pyrogallol for brown ones. One can use any dye material, however, even tea or bouillon for subtle effects. Staining presents a reason to try to get fine bubbles in the glaze, for if the bubbles in the glaze are too large, the stain will penetrate into them and produce lumpy looking lines.

So, here we are with a thick, crackled, underfired glaze on top of a thin, dark, underfired body. The net result is a ceramic that goes "thunk" when it is struck.

This is a peculiarity of several Sung ceramics. Sung potters certainly had the know-how, and equipment, and material to make porcelains. They had bodies that were quite white; they had the kilns and techniques to fire up to cone 12; and they had appropriate glaze compositions. Yet, certain wares were intentionally made with dark bodies and were intentionally underfired even though the pieces were intended for the most important clients (the Imperial Household).

This situation results in the anomaly of Kuan ceramics being classified as porcelain even though they have **none** of the criteria of porcelain (not white, not translucent, and not resonant). And yet, when confronted with a Kuan specimen, one is not shocked by the porcelain appellation, because the **effect** is that of porcelain. This result is due to the thickness and translucency of the glaze, which, because of its depth, imparts a translucency to the whole piece.

To summarize, Southern Sung Kuan ceramics are:

1. Thin bodied.

2. Dark bodied.

3. Underfired.

4. Thickly glazed via multi-layers.

5. Crackled.

6. Pale colored, usually green or blue, but sometimes cream.

CHAPTER 10

CH'AI AND JU WARE

Ch'ai ware is commonly given short shrift by students of Chinese ceramics because there are no known pieces extant. The only reference to it is in literature of much later eras.

Ch'ai porcelain was said to be made especially for the emperor Shih-Tsung (954-9), and beside being "blue as the sky" was also "clear as a mirror, thin as paper, and resonant as a musical stone". Without worrying about its other attributes, let's only consider the possibility of a pre-Sung glaze that was sky-blue in color.

The main reason that I consider it to be a possible ceramic is that I have seen Sung Chun ceramics which were truly "as blue as the sky". Thus, it has to be admitted that the color at least was possible at that time.

Another reason for considering the Ch'ai color as possible is that a sky-blue celadon can be made today with ingredients that were available to 10th century Chinese potters. Using the proper concentrations of sand, limestone, and feldspar (with a percent of iron oxide), a brilliant sky-blue can be obtained in reduction firing. With just:

49% Potash Feldspar
30% Silica
20% Limestone
 1% Iron Oxide,

a beautiful blue can be obtained if the glaze is applied thickly. Purity of raw materials would seem to be a hang-up, but it really is not. Silica and limestone are both minerals that can be commonly found in nature in a relatively pure state, and even feldspar is not often dirty.

My final reason for believing in Ch'ai is the existance of Kuan ware. Now there is an "impossible" ceramic, and yet it exists. If I hadn't seen whole Kuan ceramics, and examined Kuan sherds, and seen pictures of Kuan ware with broken edges, I would never have believed that it was possible to make a ceramic that had a glaze thicker than the body. So, having seen one "impossible" ceramic it is not hard to adjust to the existence of other "impossible" ware.

In particular, I can conceive of two possible scenarios for making Ch'ai ware in 950 AD.

In situation one, we have a large kiln containing 10,000 celadon pieces that are normally bluish-green. These pieces were possibly glazed by 10 men over a period of 10 days. During this time the glaze slip was settling out and being stirred up again; new glaze was being ground up and added; the batch composition was varying continuously; some of the ware was bone-dry when glazed, other ware was slightly damp, so the glaze thickness was changing. Also there would be kiln temperature and atmosphere variability from top-to-bottom and from front-to-back. Out of these combinations and permutations why not select one or ten pieces that are really much bluer than any of the rest and send them to the emperor?

In situation two, I can see the kiln boss saying to his crew: "Men, the Emperor wants some blue pots. Now I don't care whether you have to tear down a mountain or fire the kiln to cone 36 but we are going to get some blue pots." (meanwhile fanning the air lightly with a bamboo cudgel). You can't beat reasoning!

There might even be a situation three, with an early Chinese Edison who noticed that his glazes got bluer as the slip level got lower in the tank.

Having convinced myself that a Ch'ai glaze could have been made, I'm quite willing to wait until a modern Chinese bridge-builder sinks a caisson into an old kiln site and gives us the real answer.

JU WARE

Ju is another rare Sung ceramic which fortunately is not as scarce as Ch'ai. There are a few dozen Ju pieces remaining in the East and the West with the finest collections located in the Percival David Foundation (London) and the National Palace Museum.

Sir Percival David described Ju ware (1) as an Imperial ceramic made from 1107 to 1127 AD, with kiln locations reported to be at Ju Chou in Honan province.

So much for the cold statistics, the ware itself is much warmer (Figure 10.1). The shapes of Ju ceramics are simple in concept and execution like many Sung pieces, and the sizes are certainly not monumental. Unlike Ting and Yueh ware, carving or molding is not used to embellish Ju pieces. What we have are simple body shapes that serve as a foil for a soft unctuous glaze. This glaze is a thick, opaque, pale blue-to-blue green color with crackle, over a body which is yellowish in color.

The Ju Chou kiln location in north China places its manufacture near the Chun kilns, but, although both Ju and Chun are blue colored celadons, there is little other physical resemblance.

Chun ware has a hares-fur appearance due to glaze unmixing, is noted for bubbliness (particularly large bubbles), is frequently very glossy, and gives the general appearance of being high fired.

(1) David, Sir Percival, "A commentary on Ju Ware", TOCS, **14**, (1936) pp. 18-69.

IRON AS A COLORANT

0.8% 1.2% 1.6%

0.4% 2.0%

SUNG
CHUN
SHERD

0.2% 2.5%

0.1% 5-3-2
+
IRON 3.0%

The base glaze in most of these plates consists of 50 parts Kona feldspar, 30 parts silica, and 20 parts limestone, all ground to 200 mesh. This composition is designated by the code (5-3-2 or 532). To achieve a celadon, one percent of an iron compound would be added and the designation would then be either 5-3-2-.1 or 532.1. If ten parts of clay were added, the designation would be 5321.1.

This first plate illustrates the fact that reduced iron in a glaze does not function like a colorant such as cobalt. At low concentrations (<1%), it is a pale blue (in the absence of titanium) but at high concentration (>2%), it becomes a dirty color rather than just a deeper blue.

The sherd found in the center of this plate is a Chinese relic dating back to about 1200 AD and illustrates the blue color obtained by these craftsmen.

CLAY IN CELADON GLAZES

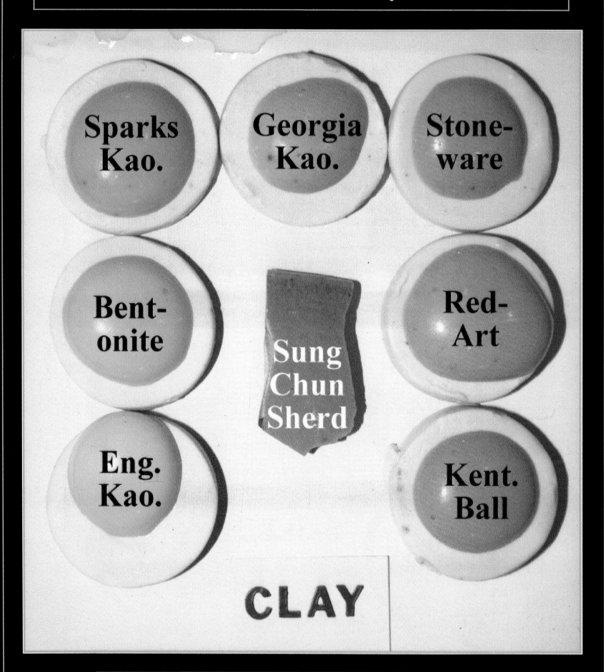

Sparks Kao.

Georgia Kao.

Stone-ware

Bent-onite

Sung Chun Sherd

Red-Art

Eng. Kao.

Kent. Ball

CLAY

Plate 2 illustrates the effect of a variety of clays on the blue celadon color. There are two functions of clay in these 5321.1 test buttons. The most important is with regard to color and is directly related to the concentration of titania in the clay. With a low titania clay such as English kaolin, the glaze remains a pale blue. However, when the clay contains a percent of titania, as in the Georgia kaolin, a green color results.

A second consequence of low clay concentrations in glazes is to prevent opalization and, as shall be shown later, it is desirable to have an opal glaze when making exquisite blue celadons.

ALKALINE EARTHS IN CELADONS

In studying an unknown glaze such as an ancient Chinese celadon, one is always suspicious that some exotic material may have been used to obtain a beautiful effect.

One such possibility is that an alkaline earth element other than the usual calcium might have been obtained from a local ore. However, this set of test buttons shows that calcium is the preferred element. This also has been shown by chemical analysis of sherds of ancient celadon ceramics.

CALCIUM IN CELADONS

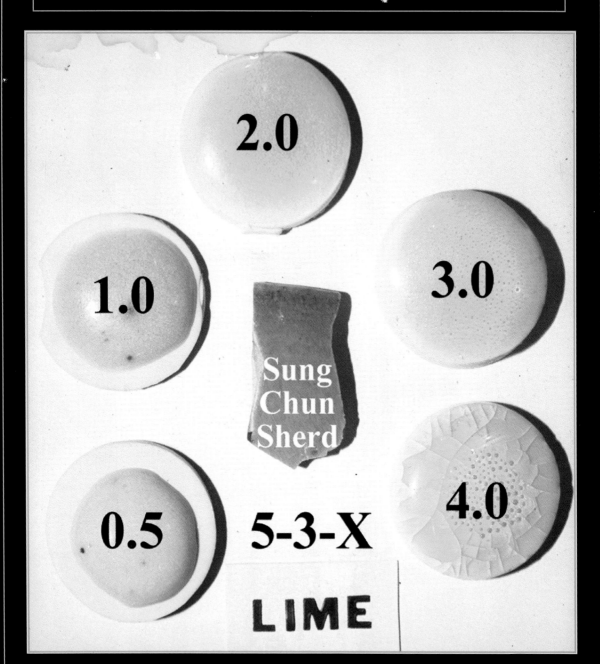

2.0

1.0

3.0

Sung
Chun
Sherd

0.5

5-3-X

4.0

LIME

Since we have seen that calcium is the preferred flux for blue celadons, the next question is, "What is the preferred concentration of calcium for the best blue color?"

Plate 4 shows the gradation in blue as the glaze progresses from one containing too little calcium to one containing too much. A subsidiary effect is the presence of numerous bubbles and much crazing in the glaze with the highest calcium content.

ALKALIS AND CELADONS

Buck. Spar

Corn-wall

Lepid-olite

Kona Spar

Spod-umene

Sung Chun Sherd

Soda Spar

Petalite

5-3-2

Neph. Sye.

ALKALI

FELDSPAR IN CELADONS

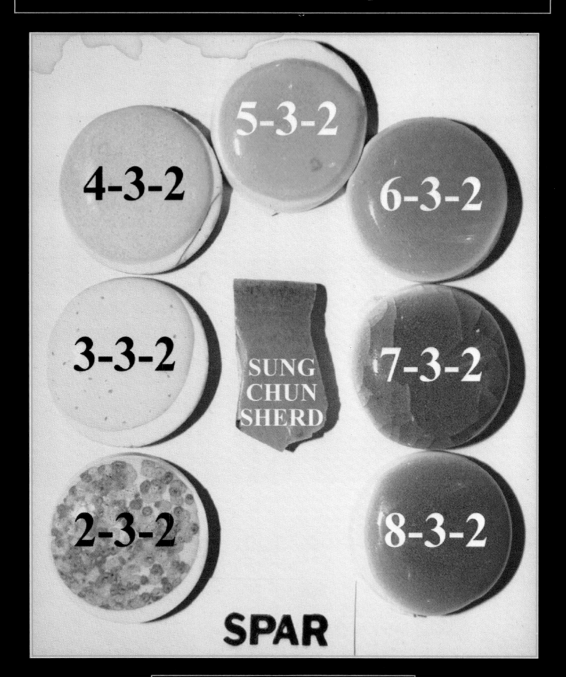

4-3-2
5-3-2
6-3-2
3-3-2
SUNG CHUN SHERD
7-3-2
2-3-2
8-3-2
SPAR

Since we have found that a potash spar is the best source of alkalis, the next question is, "How much feldspar should be used?"

Plate 6 demonstrates the results obtained from varying the Kona spar in a 532.1 glaze. Proceding from 2 to 8, it is obvious that, as usual, there is a golden mean and it is not far from the 50% level.

SILICA IN CELADONS

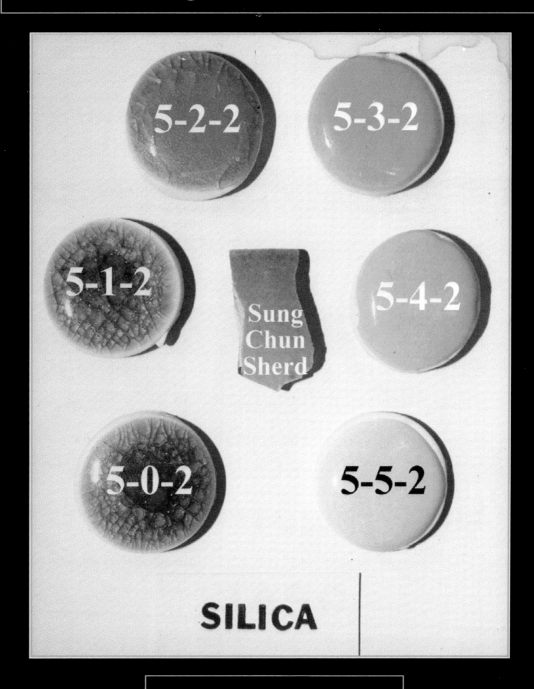

5-2-2

5-3-2

5-1-2

Sung
Chun
Sherd

5-4-2

5-0-2

5-5-2

SILICA

This next test changes the silica level in our standard 532.1 glaze from 0-5 and once more locates a mean level for good blues.

Silica is acting as an opalizing agent and at high concentrations, the glaze becomes so opalescent that the blue color is washed out.

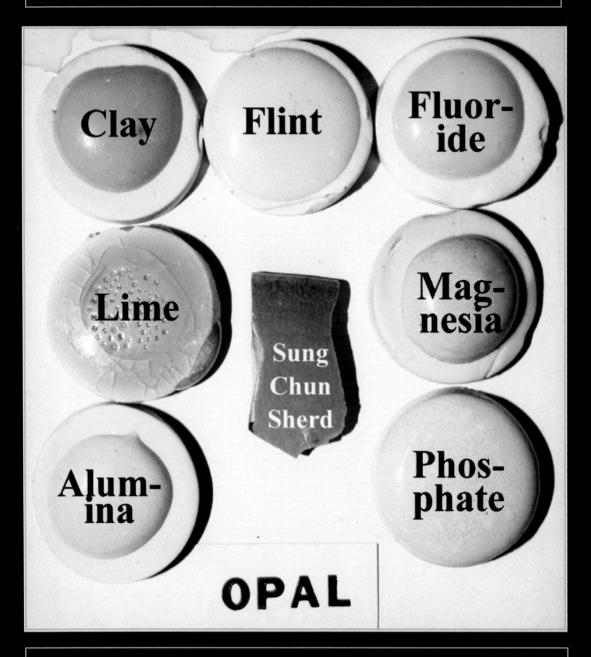

Clay — Flint — Fluor-ide — Lime — Sung Chun Sherd — Mag-nesia — Alum-ina — Phos-phate — OPAL

The role of opalescence in celadons is subtle but important. Opals can be generated by several techniques. Ordinary materials can produce opals if they are used in the correct concentrations. These concentrations can vary widely, since it only takes about 1% phosphate to form an opal, while it takes about 20% lime to make one.

A point of further interest is that a combination of two materials can give an opal using lower concentrations than would be expected from each acting alone. A case in point deals with silica and phosphate. A glaze with a high (but not opalescent) silica content can be driven to opalescence by a rather small addition of phosphate.

Plate 8 shows opals generated by seven different additions (widely different in concentration). Fluoride, magnesia, and alumina (as pure alumina) were not used by the Sung dynasty Chinese, as determined by chemical analyses. Lime, clay, flint, and phosphate were definitely part of the ancient celadons. The phosphate was no doubt the consequence of ash being used as a flux in these glazes.

QUENCHING CELADONS

It is fortunate that ceramic firing takes place the way it does. Ware is fired to a very high temperature and then is cooled at a slow rate to a relatively cool temperature before removal from the kiln. This procedure is perfect for producing opals as it allows a liquid or crystalline phase to separate in the glaze. While one would not normally remove a red hot ceramic from a kiln, a test of this process is illustrated in Plate 9 by three identical glazes.

One button was fired to cone 10 and was allowed to cool at the furnace rate. It opalized when cooling slowly and produced a desirable celadon blue. The other two pieces were fired to cones 12 and 14 and were removed at the highest temperature and plunged into cold water. This rapid quench froze the glazes in the glassy state and prevented opal formation and good blue colors.

One thought provoked by this test is that if slow cooling in a modern kiln produces a certain degree of opalizing, what effect would have been produced in ancient kilns which were heated slowly for days and then cooled slowly for days? We may expect to approach the type of glazes produced by the Sung Chinese, but we will probably never match them.

GREEN CELADONS

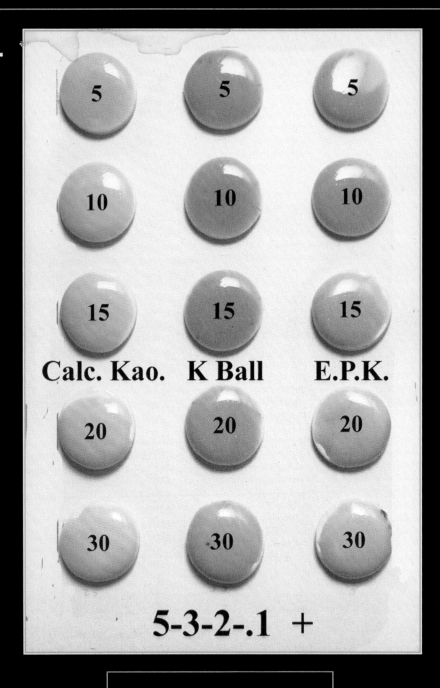

Calc. Kao.	K Ball	E.P.K.
5	5	5
10	10	10
15	15	15
20	20	20
30	30	30

5-3-2-.1 +

There were many lovely green celadons produced by the Sung Chinese, especially in Lung-ch'uan. Here are some colors of this type produced by adding the percentage of clays specified in a base glaze of the standard 50-30-20-1 type. This variety of color covers much of the range seen in the Chinese types.

LIMITS TO GREEN CELADONS

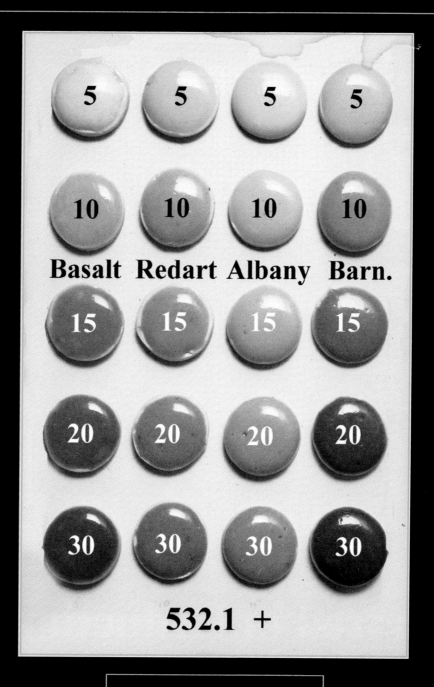

Basalt Redart Albany Barn.

532.1 +

While some clay additions will produce lovely green celadons, there are limitations. Clays or rock powders with high iron, titania, or manganese contents should be used with discretion. The clays used in this series can produce some pretty ugly glazes if they are used in high concentrations.

REDUCING FIRES AND CELADONS

Fired in Reduction

This is a trick picture, but I hope that you will forgive me because it is educational. Both of these pots were glazed with the same glaze and both were fired side-by-side in a normal reduction kiln. The trick is that the upper pot was first fired in oxidation until the glaze sealed over. Then it was fired to maturity with the lower (raw glazed) pot in a reduction fired kiln.

The point of this experiment was to prove that iron glazes are not affected by the reduction kiln atmosphere if they have once been oxidized while the glaze is open. In other words, there is no hope of converting a yellow oxidized iron glaze to a green or blue celadon by refiring it in a reducing atmosphere.

OXIDIZING FIRES AND CELADONS

Fired in Oxidation

This is another trick photograph, but with a useful purpose. Both of these pots were coated with the same glaze and both were fired side-by-side in the same oxidizing kiln.

The trick was similar, only in this case, the upper pot was first fired in reduction until the glaze sealed over. Then it was fired to maturity in an oxidizing kiln together with the other (raw glazed) pot.

This time the reduced celadon glazed pot retained its green color despite the oxidizing atmosphere. This experiment showed that the oxidizing atmosphere was not able to convert the green celadon to a yellow glaze.

The useful point of this experiment is that once a celadon glaze is sealed over, the kiln can be turned to an oxidizing state without any danger of losing the iron blue or green color. As one approaches the end of a kiln firing, it can be advantageous to go slightly oxidizing to speed up reaching the final temperature.

Fired at
Cone 10

Fired at
Cone 8

This plate illustrates the tenuous nature of glaze quality as a result of firing temperature. Once again, two pieces were made of the same body and coated with the same glaze. They were then fired separately in light reduction, one to cone 8 and the other to cone 10.

One can readily see why there is such a variation in celadon ware made in a giant Chinese kiln. Palmgren's book, Sung Sherds, illustrates this famously with the marvelous color plates of Lung-ch'uan kiln sherds. A piece fired in a cool corner of a kiln can vary markedly from one fired in a hot spot.

One can now realize that the exotic ware we see exhibited in museums today represents a manyfold selection process. The poor pieces went to the peasants, the good ones were for export, and the sensational ones were shipped to the emperor and his court. The latter ones had the best chance of surviving.

532.1
+
1 K Ball

532.1
+
1 Eng. Kao.

These two bowls are included here to demonstrate once more the elusive nature of a single type of celadon. Both glazes would be perfectly acceptable celadons, but merely a variation in the grade of clay would result in a green glaze versus a blue glaze. One can imagine the frustration that must have been the lot of the Sung potters. They were completely at the mercy of the party who dug the clay. To a small extent, we still face this dilemma, but it is many degrees less than it once was. Clays are probably one of the most variable commercial minerals in production and you ignore this fact at your own risk.

A KUAN REPLICA

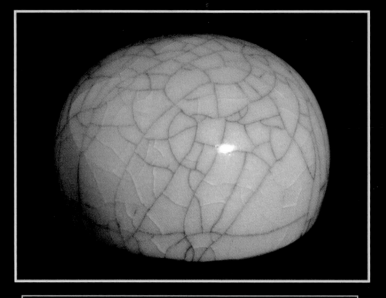

One of the easiest Sung glazes to replicate is the Kuan. The only difficulty is in getting the glaze thick enough and in firing it to just the right temperature.

A CHUN REPLICA

Another easy Sung type glaze is the Chun. One only has to be carefeul and not overdo the phosphate content. The copper splash procedure is also tricky and the result is invariably a surprise with regard to color. The splash can easily vary from deep blue to a delectable plum color.

Courtesy of the Percival David Foundation of Chinese Art.

Figure 10.1. Ju ware bowl. Sung dynasty.

Ju on the other hand physically resembles Kuan ware in that it appears to be underfired, having a faintly crystalline, sugary appearance as opposed to the Chun opalness. Unfortunately there are no Ju sherds, so analytical evidence is not available for comparative purposes. Until a non-destructive analytical test, such as non-dispersive X-ray analysis is performed on a Ju piece, we can do no better than speculate.

If I were to try to make a Ju-type glaze I would go the Kuan-route, making a glaze with a feldspathic base, some iron oxide colorant, perhaps a small amount of clay to bring the color off pure blue, and a high lime content (15-20% CaO). Then I would underfire the glaze to promote opacity and crackle.

Throwing the Ware.

CHAPTER 11

CHIEN-TEMMOKU

Figure 11.1   Map of China

First, we need to get the nomenclature straightened out with these ceramics, is it Chien or is it Temmoku? Chien is a place name in Fukien province (Figure 11.1) near the sites where the bowls were made in the Sung dynasty.

Thus "Chien ware" is an accurate description of a particular kind of ceramics (Figure 11.2) and separates this ware from confusion with the similar pieces made in northern China at the same time. The term Temmoku on the other hand, is a Japanese expression derived from the name "T'ien Mu Shan" (Mountain of the Eye of Heaven), the location of a monastery in Chekiang province where a tea ritual was performed using Chien bowls. Chien bowls that were taken to Japan from this monastery were then known as Ten-moku or Temmoku. One drawback to the Temmoku name is that it was also used to describe pieces made in the North China provinces of Hopei and Honan. Since these were made using white clay bodies, they have only a superficial resemblance to Chien ware (Figure 11.3). Nevertheless, following the lead of Plumer (1), who located the actual kiln sites, we will use the terms interchangeably.

---

(1) Temmoku — A Study of the Ware of Chien — J.M. Plumer — (1972) Idemitsu — Tokyo

**Figure 11.2. Temmoku bowl
with Hare's Fur glaze.**

Courtesy: The Metropolitan Museum of Art. Bequest of Edward C. Moore, 1891. (91.1.226)

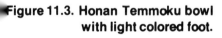

**Figure 11.3. Honan Temmoku bowl
with light colored foot.**

Oil Spot (Figure 11.4), Hare's Fur (Figure 11.2), Partridge Feather, Khaki, Yohen, and all of the other variations in glaze effect must have resulted from slight differences in raw materials, time, temperature, or atmosphere in the kiln. To try for one particular variant of color might very well be a fool's errand, even with today's tight control of raw materials and kiln variables. One feels that the proper way to make ware like Chien-temmokus is to place the bowls in the kiln, fire away, and trust to kiln placement and firing to give the different variations of color and pattern.

Having settled on the name, Chien-Temmoku, what is the ware itself like? It is a **peasant** ceramic, but what a great ceramic! It is not a typical, fragile, underfired piece of porous clay, it is a robust, high-fired, dense stoneware like no other kind.

It is certainly not delicate! Holding a Chien bowl is like handling a piece of bronze. The body is so dense and the glaze so thick, it seems impossible for it to be made of common clay. The dark coarse body is unlike any in the world before or since. And one instinctively feels that there was no subtlety used in compounding this body. This was not blended, or screened, or meagred. It must have been dug straight from the earth underfoot, and been thrown directly into bowls.

The Chien glaze is only slightly more refined than the body. All the months that I was trying to duplicate the hare's-fur glaze, I felt that the glaze must be made up of just one or two components. It was with a feeling of real relief that the final recipe turned out to be just a mixture of red clay and wood ash. This glaze gives the dark brown, almost black color with the bluish iridescence. It also forms the subtle streaks and spots of the hare's-fur and the partridge feather. Even more exciting, this glaze has the same microscopic appearance and x-ray pattern as the original.

Courtesy: The Smithsonian Institution, Freer Gallery of Art, Washington, D.C. (09.369)

Figure 11.4.

Chien "Oil-spot' Temmoku.

Making the body is the difficult part of Chien ware replication. The body is coarse, and refractory, and ferruginous. And, although materials like this probably exist worldwide they would not be mined commercially today because there is no other application for such material. We are therefore forced to compound a body, perhaps using a coarse fire clay or a sagger clay and adding an iron-rich material like Black-bird slip clay or simply ferric oxide.

Firing Temmoku reproductions is rather straight forward. Because of the high iron content of the body it must be fired in oxidation* otherwise the body iron would cause slumping. Other than that the firing must be carried to very high temperatures (cone 8-12) in order to densify the body to a cast-iron-like condition. The temperature cannot be specified because the final criterion is to obtain a runny glaze which drips off the outside of the bowls and pools up in the interior. Just as with Lung-ch'uan ware, the Chien losses must have been high as evidenced by the mountainous sherd heaps illustrated in Plumer's book.

Whereas other Sung ceramics of a given type were made in a great variety of shapes and sizes and designs Chien-Temmoku consists mainly of bowls. Also, these bowls were made principally in one comfortable, hand-size just right for a serving of rice or tea. There are some mini-bowls and some "Giants", but most are 3-5 inches in diameter.

There are several silhouettes basic to Chien ware (Figure 11.6) but one common shape is rather classic and is definitely unique to this region (Figure 11.7). In this style there is a finger groove near the rim to allow the hand to grasp the bowl solidly (especially with greasy fingers). Also there is a very cleverly designed shoulder near the base. This angled cut serves the purpose of collecting the dripping glaze into a fat roll or into beads and drops. The slant of the cut is calculated to prevent the glaze from flowing along the body down to the foot. The bowls are obviously dipped into the glaze slip only up to the vertex of this body angle.

*Presumably fuel-fired rather than electrically fired in order to maintain a 1-5% oxygen level instead of the 20% oxygen level in air.

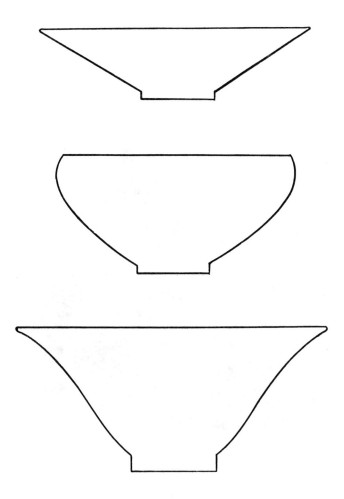

Figure 11.6. Some Chien Temmoku shapes.

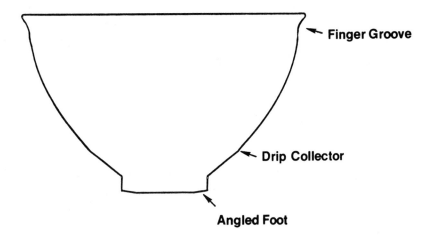

Finger Groove

Drip Collector

Angled Foot

Figure 11.7. Cross-section of a classic Chien Temmoku tea bowl.

Figure 11.8. Foot of Chien Temmoku bowl illustrating the cone-shaped base with shallow indentation.

The one fault in these bowls is the rim which is usually almost bare of glaze because of flow during firing. Also, these bare rims are quite rough since the glaze corrodes the coarse body leaving a skeleton of siliceous fragments at the surface. Later generations have often concealed the rim with a copper or silver band.

The foot of a Chien piece is its trademark when compared to a Northern Temmoku. The foot exposes the texture and color of the body and also an unusual shape (Figure 11.8). The central indentation is shallow and the foot rim is frequently tapered to a shallow cone-shape, so that the foot does not rest flat against a surface.

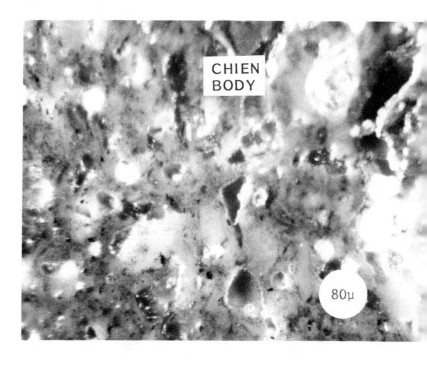

CHIEN BODY

80μ

Figure 11.9.

Optical micrograph of Chien Tommoku body in cross-section using incident light. (150 x)

Analysis of sherds via microscopy and energy-dispersive x-ray analysis has been invaluable in solving the mystery of Chien ceramics.

Starting from the bottom up a close observation of the body in cross-section using optical microscopy (Figure 11.9) reveals that it is not uniformly brown or black but is rather a dirty white sprinkled with black specks. Evidently much of the body's apparent black color is due to the thoroughness with which it was fired.*

*This is a strange effect, but really quite common. It is like a lake with a dark bottom which appears black when liquid (equivalent to a glaze) or white when frozen and covered with snow (finely crystalline). A dirty clay body appears lighter in color when finely crystalline, but darker as it becomes glassy.

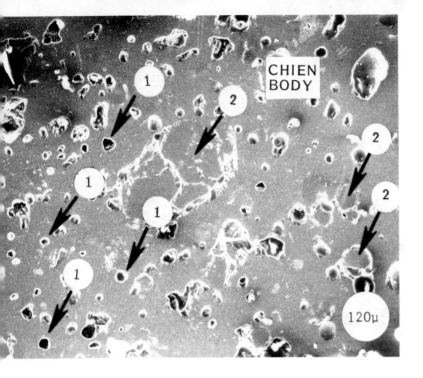

CHIEN BODY

120μ

Figure 11.10. SEM of Chien Tommoku body in cross-section showing numerous round voids (1) and silica particles (2). (100 x)

Figure 11.10 also emphasizes this point, for though the body is full of voids, they are quite round indicating that the body is well fused. It almost resembles a glaze with its high degree of blending.

116

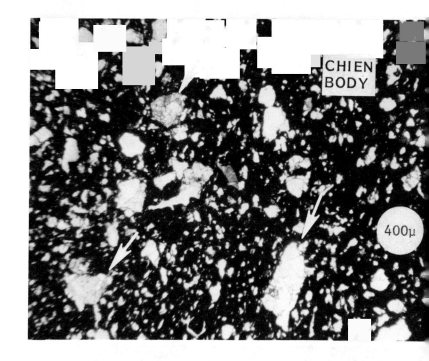

CHIEN
BODY

400μ

**Figure 11.11 Optical micrograph of Chien
Temmoku body in thin-section with
polarized light showing numerous
large quartz particles. (arrows) (35 x)**

An optical micrograph of a body thin-section (Figure 11.11)
under crossed polarizers illustrates the presence of many large
quartz grains that contribute coarseness to the body. There are
also iron-rich clay particles, fine mullite crystals, and small iron
oxide particles.

117

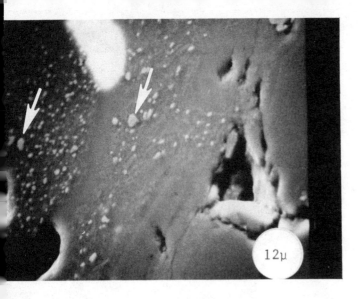

Figure 11.12. SEM of Chien body showing iron-rich particles. (1050x)

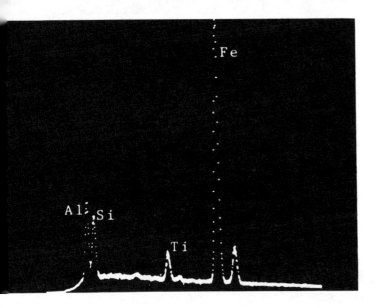

Figure 11.13. EDXR spectrum of iron-rich particle in figure 6.

Scanning electron micrographs also show iron-rich particles (Figure 11.12) which can be identified as such by energy dispersive x-ray analysis (Figure 11.13).

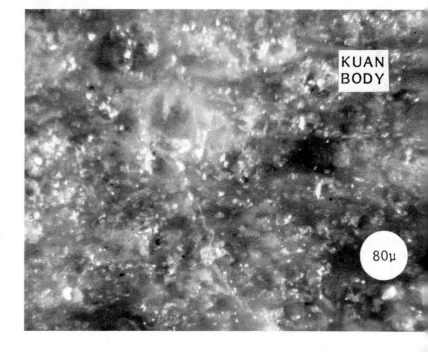

KUAN BODY

80μ

Figure 11.14. Optical micrograph of dark Kuan body (150x) illustrating uniform grey coloring.

The fact that the body iron (probably oxide) is found in fine discrete particles is a hint of the use of oxidation firing for Chien ware. If reduction had been used ferrous oxide would have functioned as a flux at high temperatures and would then have melted and blended with the clay, feldspar, and flint. For example, one does not notice fine iron particles in reduction fired dark Kuan bodies (Figure 11.14).

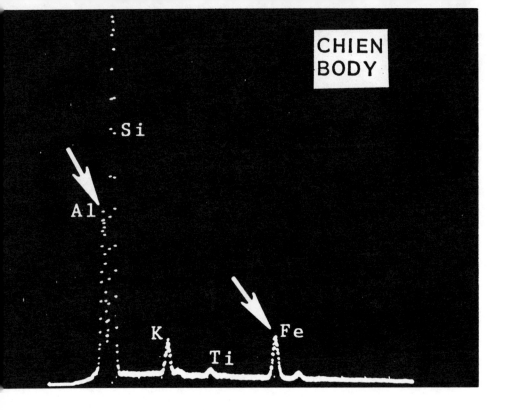

Figure 11.15. EDXR spectrum of Chien body with a high alumina and iron content.

An energy dispersive x-ray scan of the whole body area (Figure 11.15) reveals that its composition is moderately high in alumina and potash and except for a higher iron content is not much different chemically from a Chun body (Fig. 7.6), a Northern celadon body (Fig. 8.4) or a North American fire clay (Figure 11.16). Furthermore, the Chien body has only a higher alumina content than a local New York State subsoil derived from shale. (Figure 11.17). These are the reasons that point to a single local clay bed as the source for the Chien body.

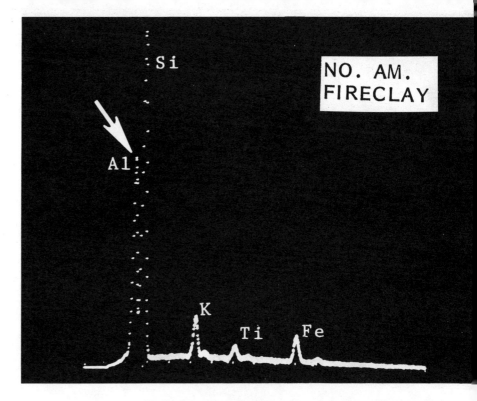

Figure 11.16. EDXR spectrum of North American fire clay with high alumina content.

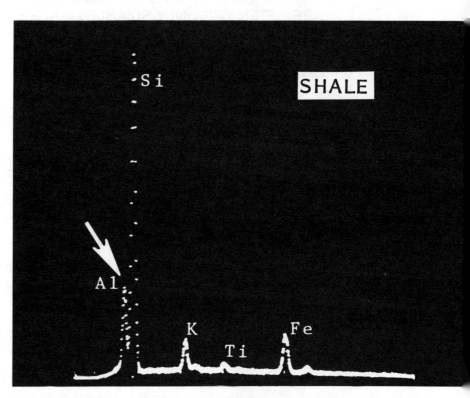

Figure 11.17. EDXR Spectrum of Devonian shale derived subsoil with a low alumina level.

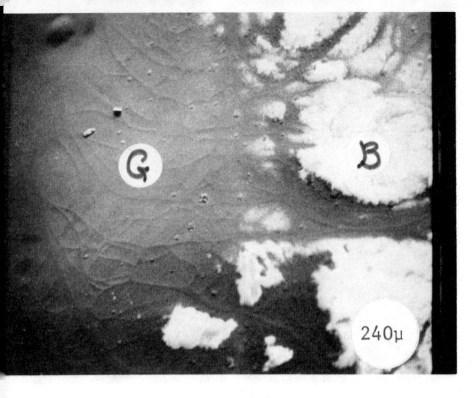

Figure 11.19.
SEM of Oil-Spot glaze surface with black glass "G" and brown spot "B". (53 x)

Turning to analyse the glaze, we first observe the drips and rolls coming off the body angle (Figures 11.2, 11.4 and 11.8). This presents a case which is well worth studying. SUCH DROPLETS ARE OFTEN THE ONLY SIZABLE GLAZE SAMPLES AVAILABLE FOR ANALYSIS. But, if we think for a moment, we realize that the compositions of such drips are really not representative of the glaze as a whole. In fact only some accidental (and small) area will represent the true glaze composition. So all of our analyses of glaze regions can only represent limits toward which direction the true glaze formula lies.

Consider the following situations on a Chien bowl:

1. Near the lip of the bowl the glaze is thin and has strongly attacked the body, hence it is higher in alumina and silica than the starting formula.

2. Near the base of the bowl the drips represent the most fluid ingredients, thus this portion will be higher in lime and alkalies.

3. At the center of the bowl on the surface the glaze has lost volatile components, so it may be low in alkali.

4. Finally, analyses of dark and light regions of surface streaks definitely shows a wide range of iron content at the surface (Figures 11.19, 11.20, and 11.21).

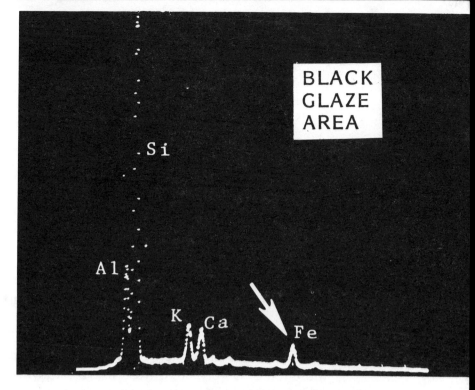

Figure 11.20.   EDXR spectrum of black glaze area "G".

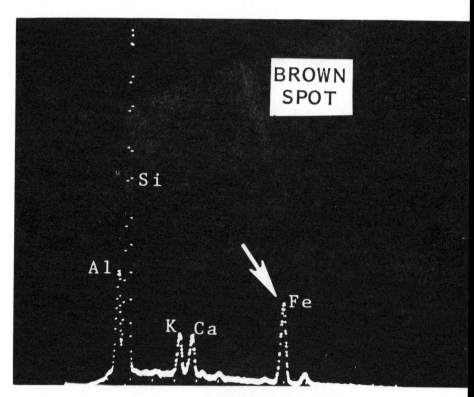

Figure 11.21.   EDXR spectrum of brown spot in area "B". Note high Fe level.

The lesson to be learned is that one should beware of glaze analyses. Even when they are completely accurate they can only represent an approximate formula for the starting glaze, because of local composition variations.

Synthesis can often be a useful analytical aid, and the formulation of Chien-like glazes was a total vindication for synthesis as such a tool. We can analyse, analyse, and re-analyse glazes and bodies, but until the numbers are tested by synthesis, they are just that, merely numbers and not real substance.

Originally reasoning that Chien glazes were made with some kind of a dark clay raw material, I tried Barnard clay, Red-art clay, local shale, and Albany slip clay, because they all had high iron contents. Of these Red-art seemed to come the closest to Chien. But, no matter how the lime, feldspar and silica content were varied to match published analyses, the glazes never came very close to the real thing except for isolated patches.

The solution to the problem came quite by accident. After analysing a series of ash samples for another project the thought occurred that since wood ashes are composed of potash and lime in nearly equal proportions, why not try just ash and Red-art clay as a glaze mixture. Luckily that happened to be the solution (in conjunction with oxidizing firing). Before that test I had just been trying all kinds of mixtures vainly hoping to match an analysis.

What makes Red-art clay and ash so special? I don't know. Perhaps it is the soluble potash in ash or maybe the phosphate in ash is critical. Local shale functions almost as well as Red-art so it seems that ash is the essential ingredient.

The degree to which ash glazes are ball-milled has an effect on the streaking and spotting of the finished glaze. Also, since the composition of wood ash varies widely this too may account for some of the differences of the Chien ware between oil spot, hare's fur, and partridge feather. Firing time and temperature are critical here also.

Chien glazes in situ on the body appear dark brown or black. However, a chip of this glaze removed and placed against a white background proves to be amber. The analogy for this can be found in an artificial pool filled with water. If the pool lining is white, then the water looks pale blue or green, but if the pool is painted black, as for a reflecting pool, then the water looks jet black. Thus if you want weak coffee to look strong serve it in dark colored cups, and if you want a pale glaze to look black put it on a dark body.

Another quirk of the Chien glaze is that the light colored spots or streaks are found to be higher in iron content than the dark glassy areas (Figures 11.20 and 11.21). This is a case where the high iron concentration has lead to surface crystallization and these crystals on the glaze make it look lighter in color.

**Figure 11.22. Photograph of inside surface of bowl
glazed with red clay-wood ash slip.**

To test and compare my formulation, a sample glaze was made with 80 parts Red-art clay and 12 parts wood ash, and this was oxidatively fired to 1250° C. on a body made up of 75 parts fire-clay and 25 parts Barnard slip clay. The resulting partridge feather glaze (Figure 11.22) was then made into a thin section for microscopic observation (Figure 11.23).

It was found to compare closely with the thin section of a Chien Temmoku oil spot glaze section (Figure 11.24). The most interesting point of similarity was the appearance of fine needle-like crystals (possibly mullite) in both glazes.

Figure 11.23.

    Optical micrograph of cross-section
of my Temmoku body and glaze. Thin-
section (200 x)

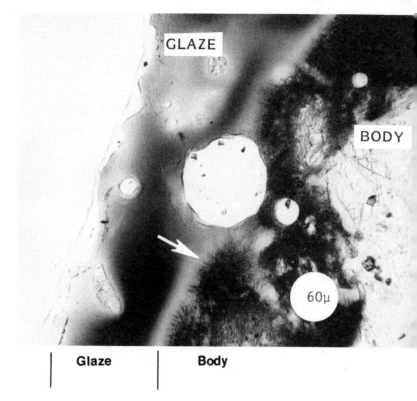

Figure 11.24.

    Optical micrograph of cross-section
of Chien body and glaze. Thin-section
(150 x)

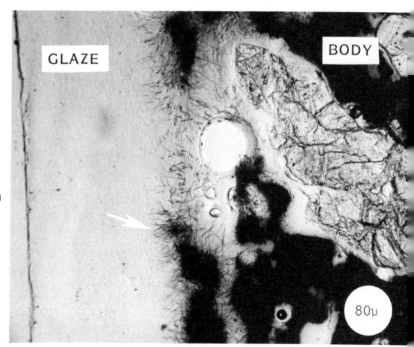

My interpretation of Figure 11.24 is as follows:

1. Since the glaze is clear and free of bubbles, and silica fragments, this means it was fired to a high temperature.

2. This is particularly true since the glaze is not high in lime content. (Figure 11.20).

3. The large quartz crystal on the right has not reacted to form crystals with the glaze.

4. The fine needle-like crystals growing from the clay-rich body into the glaze are probably mullite.

In summary, Chien Temmoku ware is a special combination of intimately connected body composition, glaze composition and firing technique.

The body must be coarse in texture and dark in color to provide the proper foil for the glaze, while the glaze is simply made up of wood ash and common red clay to give a free-flowing glass that is dark appearing and full of streaks. Firing is noteworthy in that it must be oxidative to prevent slumping of the iron-rich body. The time-temperature balance, as is usual in Sung glazes, is critical in order to provide the appropriate degree of streaking and dripping of the glaze.

CHAPTER 12

CH'ING-PAI WARE

Just as Yueh was the introduction to Sung celadons, so Ch'ing-pai may be looked on as the closing scene. The pale, very blue celadon consisting of a rather thin glaze over a white body, represents the disappearance of jade-like Sung celadons, and the approach of the cold, crisp Ming glazes.

Like Yueh ware, Ch'ing-pai is artistically carved and decorated, but unlike Yueh, Ch'ing-pai ware has a "pretty" color (that could stand alone). Unfortunately prettiness is not a Sung characteristic. Sung wares are bold, exotic, classic, handsome, jade-like, magnificent perhaps, but not "pretty."

An interesting aspect of Ch'ing-pai is that this glaze can be made from other Sung glazes just by a change in technique. As an example: Apply a Kuan-type glaze thinly over a white body, over-fire, and a Ch'ing-pai glaze is the result.

A whimsical possibility is that the reverse effect could probably be obtained today. One could take a pale yellow, oxidized-iron, modern porcelain glaze, and by thick application, reduction atmosphere and underfiring come up with a typical unctuous, green, Sung-like celadon.

Ch'ing-pai may be looked upon as the potter's answer to a change in society's taste. This progression in art from primitive, to moderate, to exotic seems to be ubiquitous in the course of history.

Ch'ing-pai ware is related stylistically to Northern celadons and Ting ware, but historically it seems to spring from the Ch'ing-te-chen arena. In any case, since the thin bluish glaze is dependent upon a high purity, white body, we must look on this glaze-type as representing the final chapter of the Sung ceramic era. It represents the closing of the Sung ceramic "Ring" that started with thin, green Yueh glazes; progressed through thick, blue Kuan types; and finished up with thin, blue, sophisticated Ch'ing-pai. (Figure 12.1)

Courtesy: The Metropolitan Museum of Art. Purchase: Fletcher Fund, 1925. (25.215.6)

Figure 12.1. Ch'ing-pai vase.

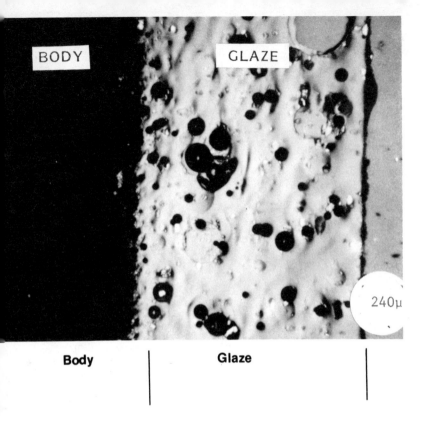

BODY   **GLAZE**

240µ

Body | **Glaze** |

Figure 12.2. Optical micrograph of Lung-ch'uan glaze. (50 x)

The technical significance of Ch'ing-pai ware is that such a glaze could never be produced over an impure body. Since it is thin and high fired, it would react strongly with the body, and any titania present in the body clay would bleed out and lead to green glaze colors.

An interesting perspective of a Ch'ing-pai sherd can be obtained by comparing it with a Lung-ch'uan sherd.

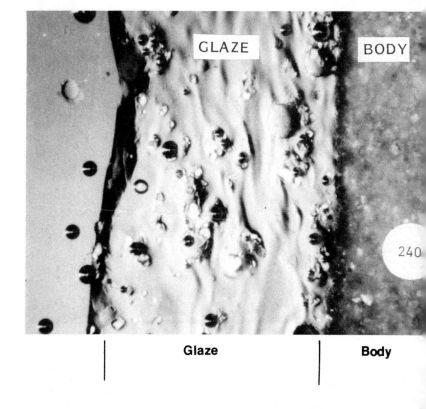

GLAZE   BODY

240

| Glaze | | Body |

Figure 12.3. Optical micrograph of Ch'ing-pai glaze. (50 x)

Optical micrographs of thin sections at low magnification (Figures 12.2 and 12.3) show the two glazes to be nearly identical in:

1. Thickness (∼lmm.)

2. Bubble density and distribution.

3. Undissolved silica relicts.

4. Flow striae.

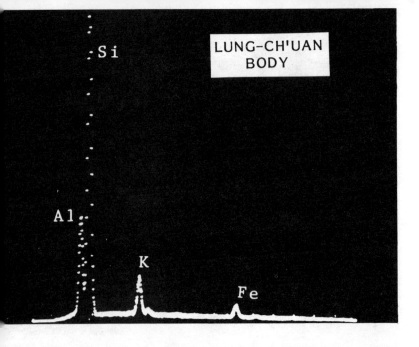

Figure 12.4. EDXR scan of Lung-ch'uan body.

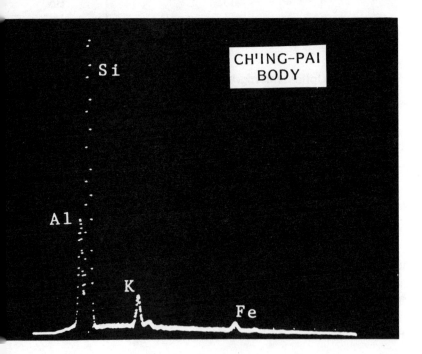

Figure 12.5. EDXR scan of Ch'ing-pai body.

Using a scanning electron microscope, EDXR traces of both **bodies** are remarkably similar (Figures 12.4 & 12.5). One notes in these results that the Ch'ing-pai body is lower in iron and potash and higher in alumina than the Lung-ch'uan, but the differences are not great.

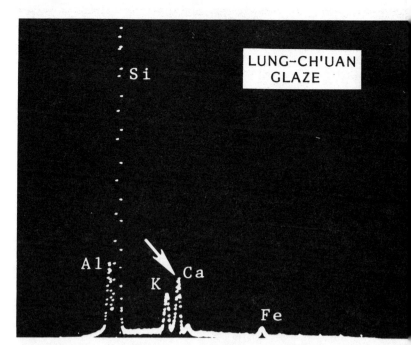

Figure 12.6. EDXR scan of Lung-ch'uan glaze.

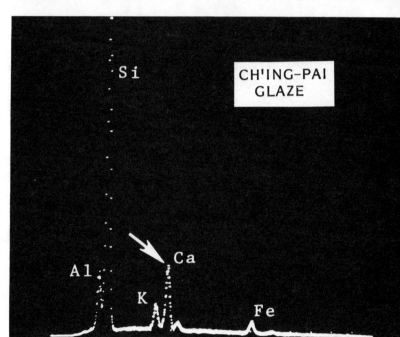

Figure 12.7. EDXR scan of Ch'ing-pai glaze.

Comparing **glazes** by EDXR (Figures 12.6 & 12.7) differences are noticeable with regard to the lime and potash percentages. The lime content is higher in the Ch'ing-pai glaze, and the lime/potash ratio is much higher for Ch'ing-pai.

Consolidating all of the analytical data on the Ch'ing-pai piece as compared with a Lung-ch'uan sherd, one notes that there is not much difference physically and chemically between the two. And yet, there is a slight chemical variation that makes a big color shift.

An era is being entered where subtle changes in technique or raw materials are going to make large variances in the end effect. Potters will no longer be able to take bank-run clay and make a body, then grind up granitic rock with ash and make a glaze.

The subtle difference is brought out by body analyses in "Sung Sherds" pp. 416 & 439. Disregarding the major constituents, let's look at the important coloring contaminants in respectively, Ch'ing-pai (Ying-ching) and Lung-ch'uan (Ta-yao) bodies.

	Ch'ing-pai	Lung-ch'uan
Ferric Oxide	0.59	2.38
Titanium Dioxide	0.06	0.18

These results represent a remarkable accomplishment in the Ch'ing-pai case. One would be very proud of such low contaminant levels in a modern body.

The low iron and titania percentages in Ch'ing-pai ensure a blue celadon in contrast to the green Lung-ch'uan celadon glaze.

This glaze, like Northern celadon must be considered a foil for underglaze carving. It is a beautiful pale blue celadon glaze, but on an undecorated piece it is only the shadow of that on a finely carved piece.

Fortunately carving does not have to be complex to be effective, so try your hand at making a few simple leaves or petals before passing up this glaze.

To make the glaze, I suggest taking the Kuan recipe (with Cornwall stone to avoid crazing) and apply it thinly. Then, overfire the glaze so that it is not bubbly and will run into the carved decorations. It may even be desirable to omit phosphate in the glaze, since in a thin layer there will be no opalization.

A major requirement is a white body with clays low in titania to accentuate blue coloration.

Otherwise, Ch'ing-pai is just a high-fired, thin Kuan glaze.

Sorting the Glaze Color.

CHAPTER 13

MICROSCOPY OF GLAZES

The microscopy of glazes is important for two reasons in the plan of this book. In the first case, microscopy is necessary to determine how the Chinese made their glazes the way they did. Obviously they did not know **why** their glazes turned out the way they did, they only knew **how** to make them that way. To emulate their glazes we must know more about both the how and the why because we lack the verbal tradition which allowed them to pass information from generation to generation orally.

Secondly, we need microscopy to use on our test results so that we can determine when we are doing the right thing and when we are doing the wrong thing in our duplication effotts.

OPTICAL MICROSCCOPY

Assuming that we know from analyses what the chemical composition of a Chinese glaze is, here are some physical things that we can learn from optical microscopy of both Sung glazes and our glazes.

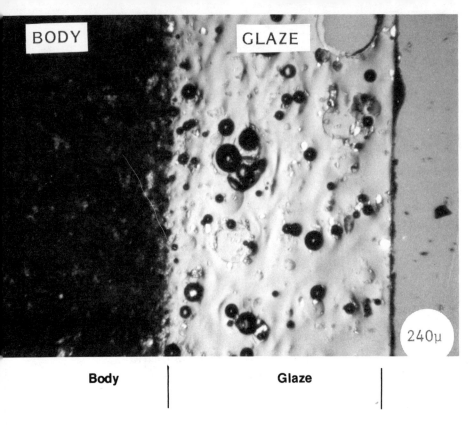

BODY   GLAZE

240µ

Body | Glaze |

**Figure 13.1. Cross-section of a typical, thick Sung
glaze (50 x) (A Lung-ch'uan celadon)**

GLAZE
THICKNESS

Although rather obvious, glaze thickness is extremely important to our efforts. It is the single most important factor in making
Sung-like glazes. Many of the beautiful Sung glazes are in the
0.5-2.0 mm thickness range (Figure 13.1), while modern commercial glazes are apt to be in the 0.1 mm class. And, since glazes on
vessels will vary from top-to-bottom, it is very useful to study this
effect and evaluate what the optimum thickness should be for
good glaze color and texture.

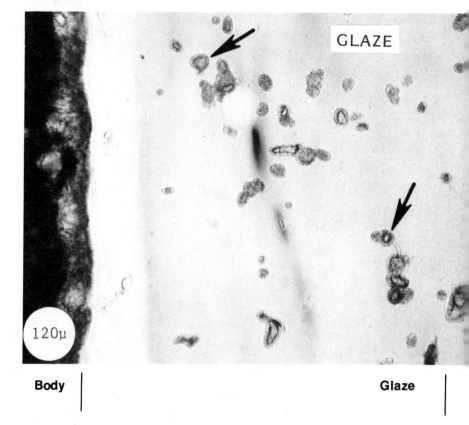

Body | **Glaze** |

Figure 13.2. A cross-section showing undissolved silica grains in a high-fired Chun glaze. (100 x)

RAW MATERIALS

Since some Sung glazes are underfired, observation of un-melted batch materials is information that can be picked up via microscopy. The presence of unmelted quartz grains has a strong opalizing effect in Chinese glazes, and this can be observed at low magnification (Figure 13.2).

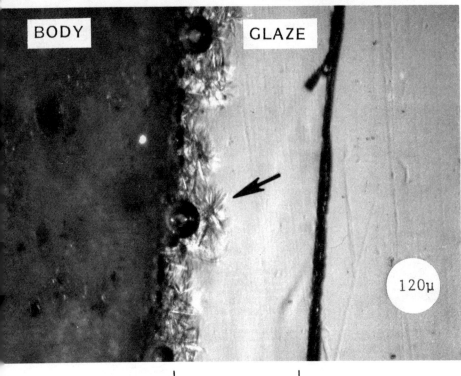

BODY   GLAZE

120μ

Body | Glaze |

Figure 13.3. Cross-section of a high-fired Northern celadon glaze with few bubbles and a crystalline glaze-body reaction layer.   (100 x)

FIRING
TEMPERATURE

Both temperature and time of firing can be judged from the crystals and bubbles present in Sung glazes. A clear glaze with few bubbles indicates high firing and slow cooling (Figure 13.3). So does a crystalline reaction zone between the body and the glaze.

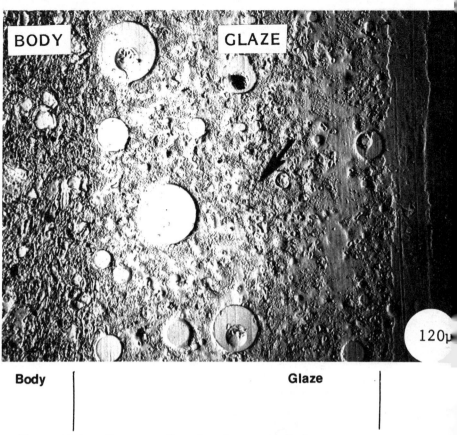

BODY GLAZE

120μ

Body | Glaze |

Figure 13.4. **Cross-section showing unreacted batch crystals in an under-fired Kuan glaze. (100 x)**

On the other hand masses of fine crystals from excess lime also indicate the degree of underfiring (Figure 13.4).

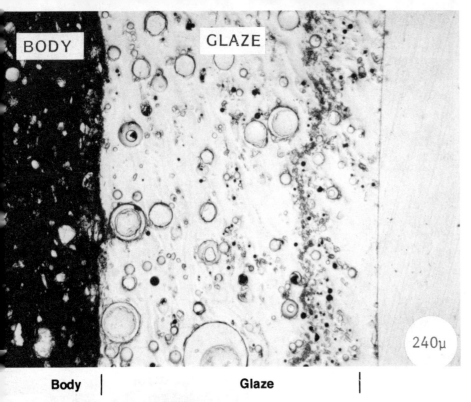

Body | Glaze |

Figure 13.5.

Cross-section showing many bubbles in an underfired Kuan glaze. (50 x)

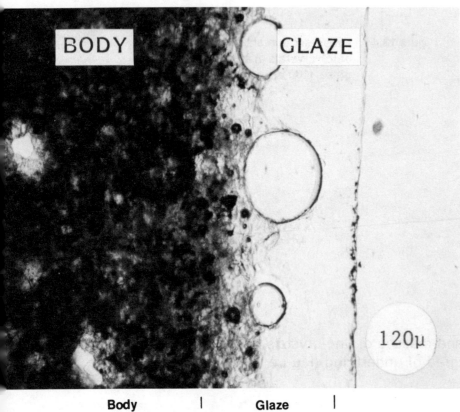

Body | Glaze |

Figure 13.6.

Cross-section of a high-fired Yueh glaze with large bubbles at the glaze-body interface (100 x)

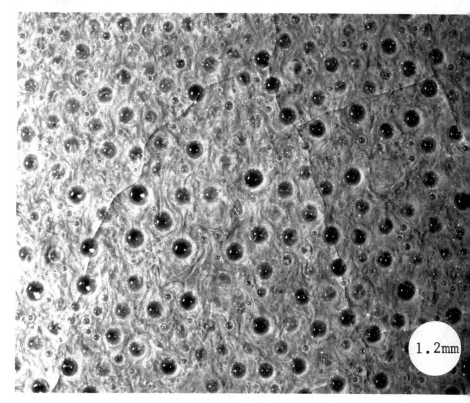

1.2mm

Figure 13.7. Bubbling at the surface of a reduced phosphatic glaze (10 x)

BUBBLES

Judgement must be used in evaluating the presence of bubbles, however. Fine bubbles well dispersed in the glaze indicate underfiring (Figure 13.5), but large bubbles at the glaze-body interface would indicate overfiring (Figure 13.6).

Also, the presence of phosphate in the glaze leads to formation of large bubbles during overfiring in reducing atmospheres (Figure 13.7).*

---

* We must remember that in the commercial process for making phosphorus, carbon reacts with sand and phosphate rock to form phosphorus, carbon monoxide, and calcium silicate; and all of these conditions can be present in the glaze environment. Another point is that the boiling point of phosphorus is 280°C.

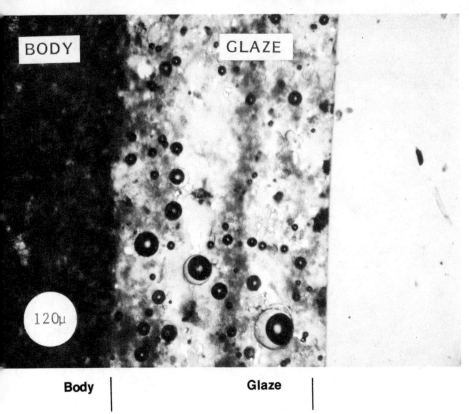

BODY   GLAZE

120μ

Body | Glaze |

**Figure 13.8.   Cross-section of a Lung-ch'uan
                celadon sherd with layered structure in
                the glaze (100 x)**

LAYERING

One of the techniques used by the Sung potters to achieve
their thick glazes was the application of 2-4 glaze layers (Figure
13.8). IN ADDITION, THE LAYERS WERE OFTEN OF DIFFERENT
COMPOSITIONS. This can readily be determined by microscopy.

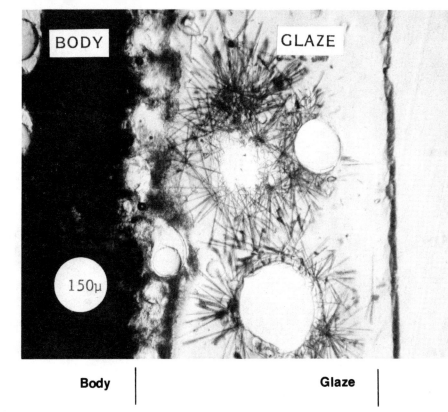

| BODY | GLAZE |

150μ

| Body | Glaze |

Figure 13.9. Cross-section of a high lime Chun glaze (80 x)

OPALIZATION

The beauty of Sung glazes is also due to the formation of opals and the cause of this can be found by microscopy. Here are four types:

a. Bubble opals (Figure 13.5) — Using a fine bubble structure to diffuse light.

b. Batch opals (Figure 13.2) — Undissolved, fine quartz particles dispersing light.

c. Crystal opals (Figure 13.9) — Excess lime in the batch leading to Wollastonite crystals.

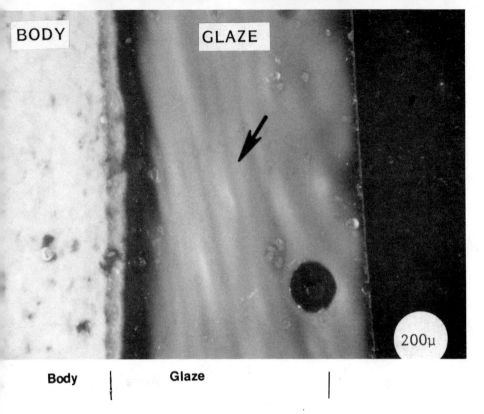

BODY   GLAZE

200μ

Body | Glaze |

**Figure 13.10. Cross-section of a high silica Chun
glaze with a smoky opal appearance.
(60 x)**

d. Glassy opals (Figure 13.10) — Phosphate present in a
low alumina glaze giving a smoky opal, blue in
reflected light and smoky brown in transmitted light.

148

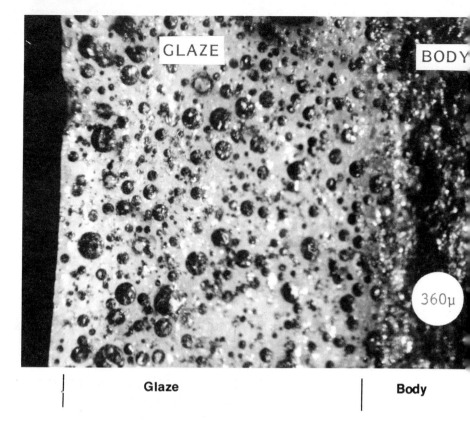

GLAZE · BODY · 360μ

| Glaze | Body |

Figure 13.11. Fracture surface of bubbly glaze filled with ink. (35 x)

One of the beauties of microscopic glaze examination is that most of the details can be observed at relatively low magnification, i.e. 10-100 x. In fact, a 10 x hand lens is adequate in many cases.

Sample preparation for observation with the microscope is more of a hold-up, since it is preferable ot examine ground and polished thin sections. Nevertheless, much can be done by pulverizing a glaze and then examining the fragments until a chip is found with the optimum thickness and covering the desired area.

Another useful trick is using ink to determine porosity in glazes (Figure 13.11). One takes a fractured glaze cross-section, rubs it briskly with a felt marking pen, wipes off the excess ink and then observes the blackened pores with a hand lens.

SCANNING ELECTRON MICROSCOPY

Shortly after beginning this work I was able to use the Corning Glass Works Scanning Electron Microscope (SEM) with Energy Dispersive X-Ray (EDXR) attachment. It was this opportunity that opened up this project and provided the basic tools that were needed for investigation. It would have been possible to work with the optical microscope and cut-and-try synthesis alone, but the SEM with EDXR provided a factor of 10 increase in information gathered per unit of time.

Optical microscopy needs little introduction because everyone has used that technique to some extent even if only with a magnifying glass.

Scanning Electron Microscopy on the other hand needs a lengthy introduction because the principles and mechanics of SEM are both unique and complicated. Unlike optical microscopy where both transmitted light and reflected light techniques are used to examine specimens, SEM is pretty much limited to the reflection mode of observation because electrons have little penetrating power in solids.

With scanning electron microscopy (SEM) we are examining specimens using a beam of electrons instead of beams of light. The principle is quite different from optical microscopy and is more related to the formation of an image by a television receiver.

First of all, SEM is a reflective type of examination because the electron beam is not able to penetrate solid objects to a size-able depth.

Secondly, scanning electron microscopy (SEM) is a vacuum operation because we are not able to manipulate beams of electrons at normal air pressures.

Third, SEM is a scanning operation because the electron beam has to search and traverse every portion of the object being examined.

And finally, SEM is a complex electronic operation because we are dealing with high voltages (20,000 V) and minute currents (micro-amperes) that must be manipulated and translated into usable optical images.

With these factors in mind let us examine the formation of a SEM image in a simplistic manner (for a full treatment refer to books on the subject by Wells (1) or Yakowitz (2)).

(1) Wells O.C. Scanning Electron Microscopy McGraw-Hill 1974.

(2) Yakowitz H. Practical Scanning Electron Microscopy

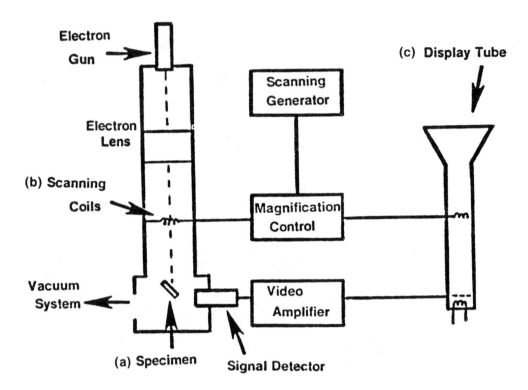

**Figure 13.12. Abbreviated schematic diagram of a
Scanning Electron Microscope.**

The SEM is basically a large demountable vacuum tube
(Figure 13.12). When evacuated, a beam of electrons is sent from
the filament to the specimen. Using magnetic lenses the electrons
are focused at a point on the specimen (Figure a). Next, by using
complex electronics and scan coils, the beam of electrons is
caused to search the surface of the specimen (Figure b). The secondary electrons which are emitted from the sample surface are
then picked up by a detector, and analysed by more complex
electronic circuits before being displayed on a video tube as a
picture of the sample (Figure c).

The beauty of all this electronic fol-de-rol is that the image
can be magnified or reduced by electronic means at the flick of a
switch. Also, magnification is limited only by the size of the
electron beam spot. Thus much higher magnification can be
reached than with the optical microscope. Another plus is the
great depth of focus in SEM images.

Figure 13.13.
Phase separation in a Sung Chun glaze by SEM. (10,000x)

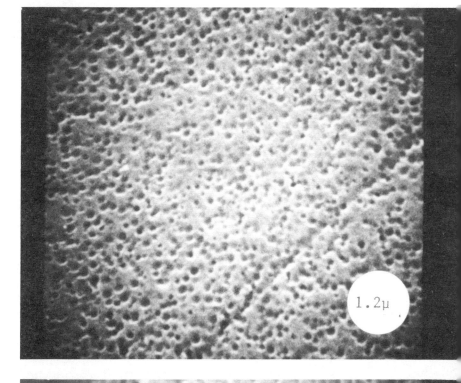

Figure 13.14.
Phase separated droplets in a replica Chun glaze by SEM. (10,000x)

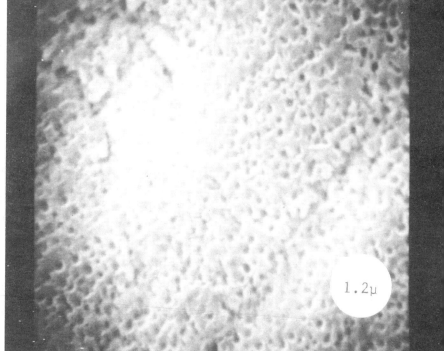

An example of the usefulness of SEM to this project can be seen in Figures 13.13 and 13.14. Figure 13.13 is a high magnification SEM of phase separation of droplets in a Sung Chun glaze which successfully identified the cause of opalization. (This detail is not resolvable by optical microscopy.) Figure 13.14 is the same kind of view of a synthetic Chun glaze, verifying that the correct duplication technique had been used.

Naturally the Scanning Electron Microscope is not without its drawbacks, and some of these are:

1. It is a vacuum device with attendent maintenance needs. Also, there are difficulties in examining hydrated samples in a vacuum.

2. It is a complex electronic device requiring continual electrical maintenance involving both skills and expense.

3. It can only examine samples by reflective modes.

4. Samples must either be electrically conducting or they must be coated with a thin conducting film.

5. SEM instruments are expensive, both to obtain and to maintain.

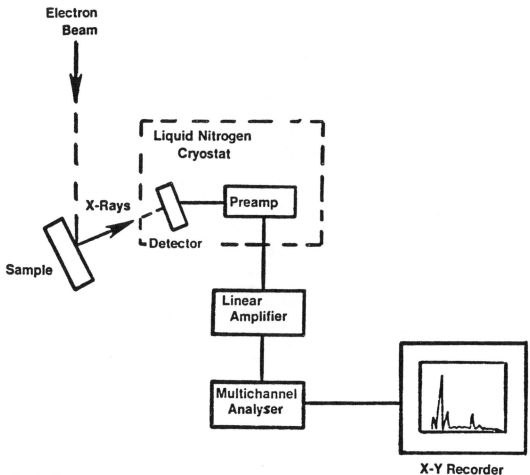

Electron Beam

Liquid Nitrogen Cryostat

X-Rays

Preamp

Detector

Sample

Linear Amplifier

Multichannel Analyser

X-Y Recorder

Figure 13.15. Block diagram of a Scanning Electron Microscope operating in the Energy Dispersive X-Ray mode.

ENERGY DISPERSIVE X-RAY ANALYSIS

Even more useful than the microscope aspect of the SEM is the potential of examining specimens by X-ray analysis. If we look at the SEM again (Figure 13.15), it is obvious that we have an X-ray generating machine at our disposal. The beam of electrons that strikes the sample not only generates secondary electrons that can be formed into an image, but it generates X-rays that are characteristic of the sample being examined. Once again, complex electronics comes to the rescue, and by very complicated techniques we are able to detect and sort the X-radiation from a sample and identify the chemical elements that it is made of. For more details of Energy Dispersive X-Ray (EDXR) techniques and mechanics consult the two references given for SEM (Yakowitz or Wells).

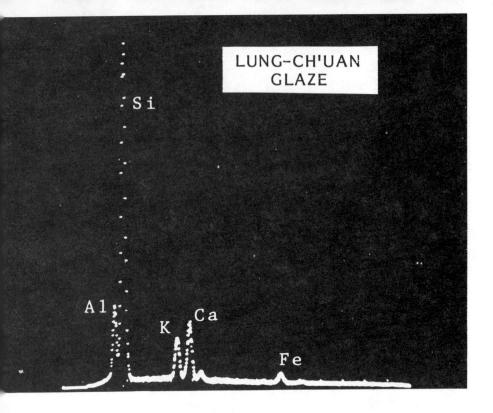

Figure 13.16. Plot of Energy Dispersive X-Ray analysis of Lung-ch'uan celadon glaze.

The information that we are interested in is that every element, when bombarded by electrons, gives off X-rays which can be characterized by their energies. For example potassium emits X-rays with energies of 3.31 and 3.59 KEV, while calcium emits 3.69 and 4.01 KEV X-rays. The complex electronic gear detects and sorts all of the generated X-radiation and displays it for us on a neat little graph (Figure 13.16). The vertical axis is calibrated in terms of the amount of X-radiation, the more radiation, the higher the peaks. The horizontal axis is graduated in terms of energies (volts). Low energy radiation is displayed toward the left and high energies to the right.

The composition of the glaze represented in Figure 13.16 is probably close to 70% silica; 15% alumina; 10% lime; 5% potash; and 1% iron oxide.

Naturally there are a few drawbacks to the EDXR system in addition to the usual maintenance problems. These are:

1. The silicon x-ray detector is located behind a thin mica window and this limits the X-rays which can escape. Only the elements sodium and above generate energetic enough X-rays to penetrate such a window. In glass research we sorely miss being able to observe lithium and boron, not to mention fluorine and oxygen.

2. As yet the ability to make precise quantitative observations is limited. The data which I have gathered gives only order-of-magnitude type information.

3. There is some interference between elements with X-rays of similar energies. This was not a problem in this work.

4. Penetration of the electron beam and the X-rays gives rise to radiation from a larger area and volume than would be expected from the electron spot size alone.

5. The silicon detector has to be maintained continually at liquid nitrogen temperatures (—195°C.).

6. EDXR has limited sensitivity. In the normal mode of operation one is not able to detect concentrations much below the 1% level.

Summing up the roles of SEM and EDXR in Sung glaze investigations — they have been powerful tools that supplemented optical observations and chemical analyses. Very simply stated, this book could not have been written without these instruments.

Painting the Ware.

CHAPTER 14

THICK GLAZES

There is one quality that distinguishes Sung ceramics from all other historical pieces — **glaze thickness.** If one compares Chun, Kuan, Lung-ch'uan, Chien, or Tz'u-chou to modern glazes, the one outstandingly different feature is thickness.

If thick glazes are examined casually, they are not impressive. After all, one merely has to apply a thicker layer of raw glaze to the body. Right? Not so right! Applying a heavy glaze layer from a viscous, dense slurry will result in a thick glaze, but only until it dries. Then one runs into cracking troubles. Fortunately this can be corrected by altering the glaze materials; for example, one can calcine the clay, or one can vary the particle size of the flint. Unfortunately this will alter the expansion or glaze color slightly, and more adjustments will then have to be made, such as changing the firing temperature and body composition.

Figure 14.1. Chun bowl with worm tracks in the glaze.

These added difficulties cannot be avoided however, because a thick glaze is absolutely necessary to reproduce most Sung glazes. One compensation is the knowledge that the Chinese potters suffered from the same difficulties. On their thick Chun pieces the presence of so-called worm-tracks (Figure 14.1) was evidence that they too had cracks in the dried glaze layer and that these healed indifferently during firing. The occasional presence of bare body (Figure 14.2) also showed that crawling due to glaze cracks was a problem for them.

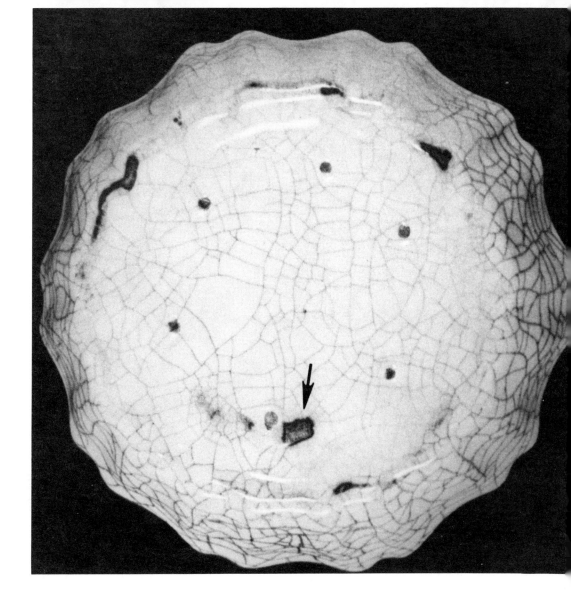

Figure 14.2. Bare body showing through a thick Kuan glaze.

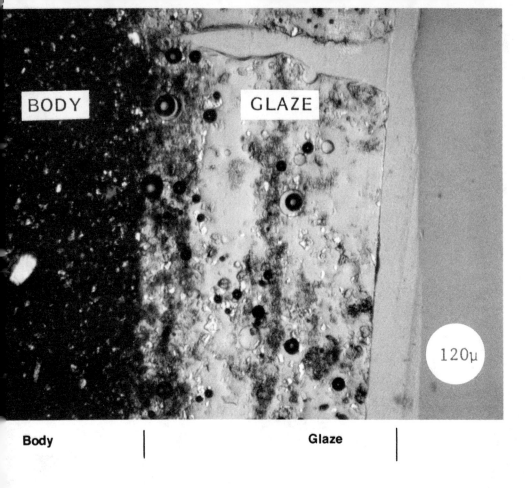

Body | Glaze |

**Figure 14.3. Optical micrograph of Lung-
ch'uan glaze cross-section
showing layering. (100x)**

Fortunately there is much internal evidence in Sung ceramics
to show how they achieved thick glazes. A prime example of this
is in Kuan ware where the presence of multiple layers is often evident at the foot rim. Layering can also be seen in Lung-ch'uan
ceramics, sometimes in an obvious second layer at the top over a
first layer covering the whole bowl, but more commonly in cross-
sectional views (Figure 14.3).

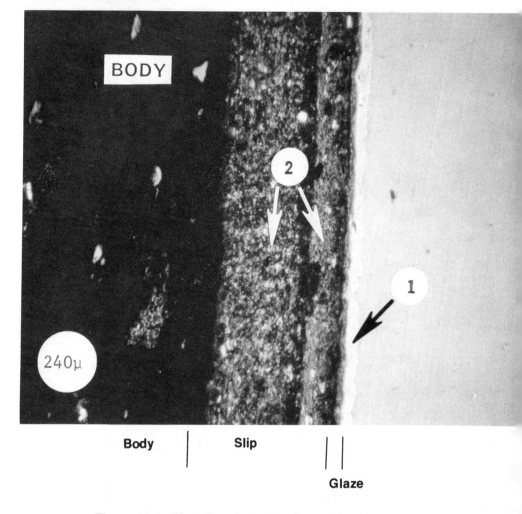

BODY

2

240μ

1

Body | Slip | Glaze

Figure 14.4. Ting-like glaze showing a thin glaze layer (1) and a double slip layer (2) over the body. (50x)

One must also consider Tz'u-chou and Ting-type ware where slips were used between glaze and body (Figure 14.4). The practice of underglaze slipping is directly related to the practice of applying multiple glaze layers. Obviously if you can master the use of a slip then you can apply the same technology to putting down two or more glaze layers.

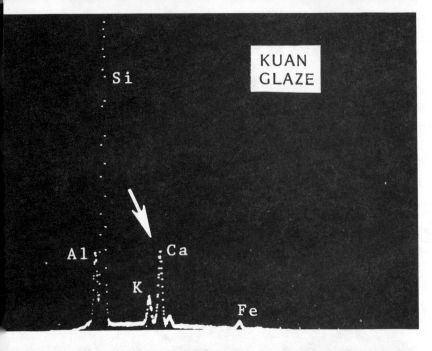

Figure 14.5.

EDXR spectrum of Kuan glaze near surface.

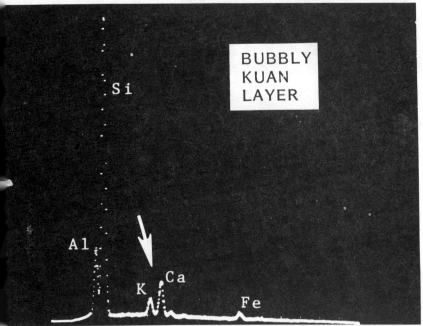

Figure 14.6.

EDXR spectrum of bubbly layer in Kuan glaze.

One interesting point on multiple glaze layers is the fact that the Chinese often used different compositions for the different layers (Figures 14.5 and 14.6). This information is available from both analysis and synthesis. The above Figures show the analytical results and experience has demonstrated the latter

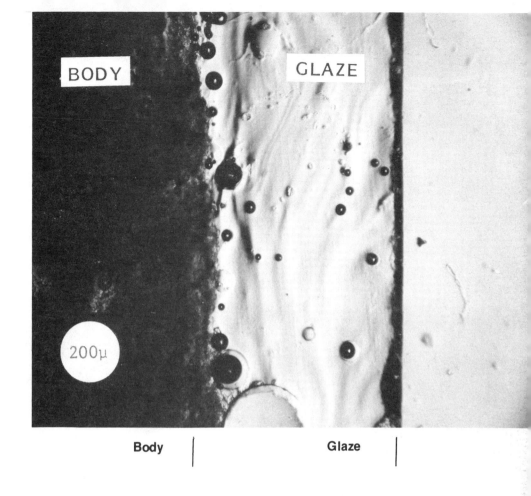

BODY   GLAZE

200μ

Body | Glaze |

Figure 14.7. Lung-ch'uan glaze with two layers blended together. (60x)

Whenever two layers of the same glaze are applied to a piece they always blend into each other, unless they are extremely underfired. If different glazes are applied to a bowl sequentially, then layering can be distinguished (Figure 14.3). An interesting case of multiple layers of a similar glaze was observed in a Lung-ch'uan celadon sherd where two layers were quite obvious externally, but on microscopic examination only a faint flow line could be noticed where the layering existed (Figure 14.7).

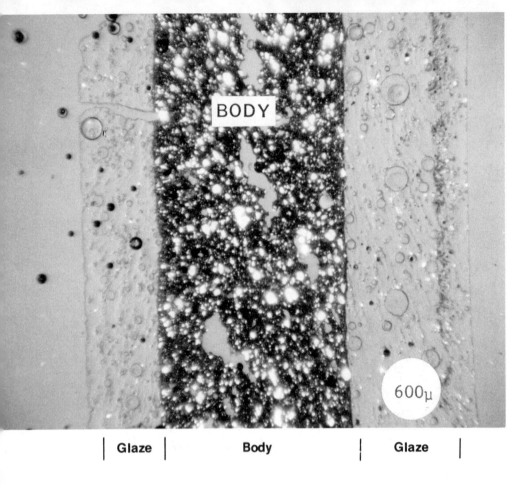

BODY

600μ

| Glaze | Body | Glaze |

Figure 14.8. Kuan sherd cross-section with unequal glaze layers. (20x)

To make thick glazes one may resort to multiple layers. And on thick bodies this may be done by dipping once, allowing the moisture to soak in the body slightly and then immediately dipping again (either in the same or a different glaze).

On thin bodies where there is not enough capacity for absorbing water from the glaze, one may dip once and then spray successive layers after enough drying has occurred. This seems to be the technique used by the Chinese on Kuan ware where the body is extremely thin. Because of this there are often great differences in thickness of glaze layers on the inside and outside of a sherd (Figure 14.8). There are also many **local** glaze thickness variations in Kuan sherds.

Whatever technique is chosen, this massiveness of glaze is a necessity if good Sung-like celadons are to be made.

166

CHAPTER 15

TEST KILNS

The most useful piece of apparatus for my experimental work has been a test kiln. For those who work with electrically heated kilns, the concept of the test kiln is a familiar one. But for the ceramist firing with gas, oil, or wood, a test kiln is not as natural. The reason for this is that with an electric kiln you can more or less set and forget it, while with a gas kiln, firing in reduction, one must constantly adjust the burners to assure appropriate firing. The problem is that it takes just as much adjusting for a small kiln as for a large one. Therefore one tends to conserve time by firing only large kilns with test samples relegated to corners of the kiln.

This is perfectly satisfactory except for one problem — the time factor. If one is developing a new glaze, the action involved is: test, then correct, test again and correct, as rapidly as possible. With large kiln firings this does not produce results fast enough. And as a corollary, it is not possible to obtain the same results by firing one lot of 500 tests as it is in firing 50 lots of 10 tests each.

In firing a small kiln 50 times, one would fire to different temperatures, for different times, with differing atmospheres. And in addition one would take the intermediate information and use it to make corrections as the tests proceeded.

Figure 15.1. Photograph of a Remmey test kiln.

Having made out a case for a test kiln, the question becomes, how to buy one or how to make one. I was fortunate in being able to buy a used Remmey test kiln that was built to fire up to cone 30. This kiln has been so useful that I will take the time to describe its features in detail.

It is a small kiln (Figure 15.1) with a door about 4″ x 6″ so that a pot about 3″ high x 3″ wide makes a satisfactory load. I have operated on natural gas at less than 6″ water pressure, but reduced to atmospheric pressure by a diaphragm. One of the great features of this kiln is that it utilizes forced air, so there is no chimney or draft needed. This means that it will fire exactly the same at —10° F or +100° F. whether it is sunny, rainy, or snowy. This feature in a test kiln is invaluable because it allows the timing variable to be kept constant and improves reproducibility from one firing to another.

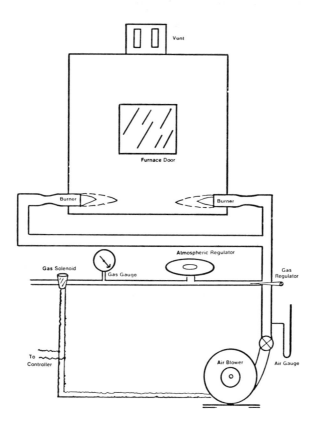

Figure 15.2. Schematic diagram of the Remmey test kiln.

The adjustments on the kiln (Figure 15.2) consist of a needle valve gas regulator and an air adjusting valve. The gas adjusting valve will maintain the redox situation at a fixed point no matter what the rate of heating. The actual rate of heating is controlled by the air valve which is only opened slightly at the start of firing and then is opened further as desired. The rate of heating is so rapid for this small kiln that usually only one adjustment is made after start-up. From a cold start, cone 8-12 will be reached in 1-1/2 to 2 hours. With a hot kiln the same temperature will be reached in 1 to 1-1/2 hours.

Cooling of the kiln takes another 1-2 hours, but I have gotten in the habit of removing samples when the temperature goes below 500°C. Since these are only tests, and all of the glazes are well set up at this temperature, a few cracks and pops are not worrisome when there is a possibility of getting in another kiln load.

By thorough drying of samples in a kitchen oven at 250°-350°F it is possible to place them directly into the 500°C kiln. They are allowed to come to thermal equilibrium in 10 minutes, then the kiln is turned on.

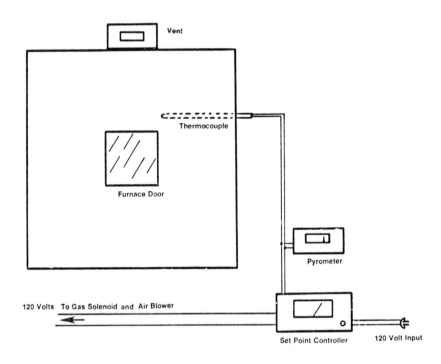

Figure 15.3. Schematic of the controls on the Remmey kiln.

To make the kiln somewhat easier to manage, the whole firing is controlled electrically. A platinum-platinum rhodium thermocouple in the kiln is connected to a pyrometer and a set-point controller (Figure 15.3). The controller is set to the desired temperature (say 1350°C) and it activates a 120 volt circuit through a relay. A solenoid on the gas line and the air blower motor are both connected to this 120 volt circuit. Thus when the controller is turned on, both the gas and air supplies go on. And, when 1350°C is reached, the relay is tripped off and both the gas and air are turned off. In case of an electrical failure the kiln turns itself off and needs to be reset to start again. If the gas should go off, the blower would continue to function, but would merely blow cold air into the kiln.

When in the throes of a glaze development, my day would be planned around four firings, at 7 AM, 12 noon, 5 PM, and 9 PM. In this way I can manage to put in a normal eight hour work day and still fire the kiln. The samples would be prepared the night before and thoroughly dried overnight at 250°-350°F.

170

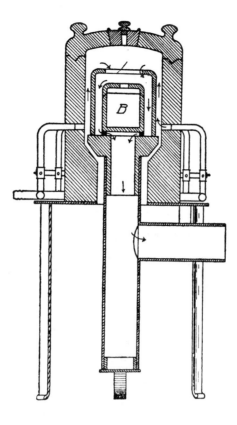

Figure 15.4. Seger's natural draft test kiln.

Normally I would have 2 parallel series of tests going on, perhaps one series on the effect of fluxes in the glaze, and another on the effect of clays in the glaze. Then if one series goes sour, a new series can be started while the alternate series is running.

Dr. Seger (1) gives the design for a natural draft test kiln (Figure 15.4) that could be adapted to modern materials and controls.

It should be possible to change a Raku design into a test kiln too, by upgrading the materials of construction and the controls. For example, the simple kiln designed by David Tell (2) would be a good starting point.

(1) Collected Writings of Hermann Seger — Chemical Publishing Company — 1902 — p. 321.

(2) Rhodes, Daniel — Kilns — Chilton — 1968.

Glazing the Ware.

CHAPTER 16

PHASE SEPARATION IN GLAZES

Phase separation deserves special consideration in this volume because it is a major factor in the uniqueness of Sung glazes. Phase separation is a principle effect in Sung celadons and yet is generally absent in both T'ang and Ming wares.

By phase separation we mean the simultaneous appearance of:

(1) a gaseous phase (bubbles) in a liquid phase (glass); or

(2) a liquid phase (droplets) in a liquid phase (glass); or

(3) a solid phase (crystals) in a liquid phase (glass.)

Common kitchen varieties of these kinds of phase separation are:

1. Meringue or whipped cream — air dispersed in a liquid.

2. Mayonnaise — Oil dispersed in an aqueous solution.

3. Fudge — Fine sugar crystals dispersed in a liquid.

The visual effect in both kitchen and glaze cases is to convert more-or-less transparent base liquids into translucent, opalescent, semi-opaque systems. The effect in Sung celadons is to change a clear, glassy-coated ceramic into a mysterious jade-like piece. The oriental admiration for jade must have been the major driving force for the development of the thick unctuous Sung celadons.

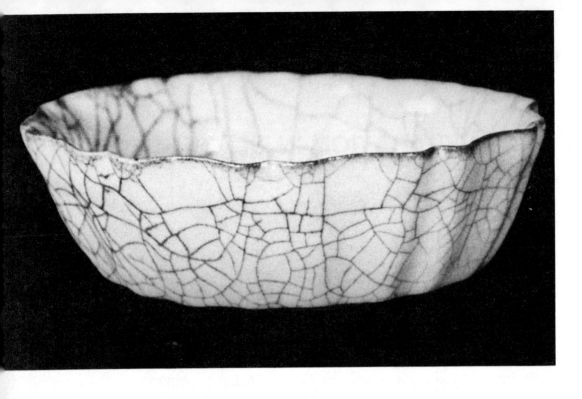

Figure 16.1. Kuan bowl. Note lack of flow in very thick glaze layer.

The most deliberate type of phase separation in Sung glazes is that due to underfiring and this is particularly noteworthy in Kuan pieces (Figure 16.1).

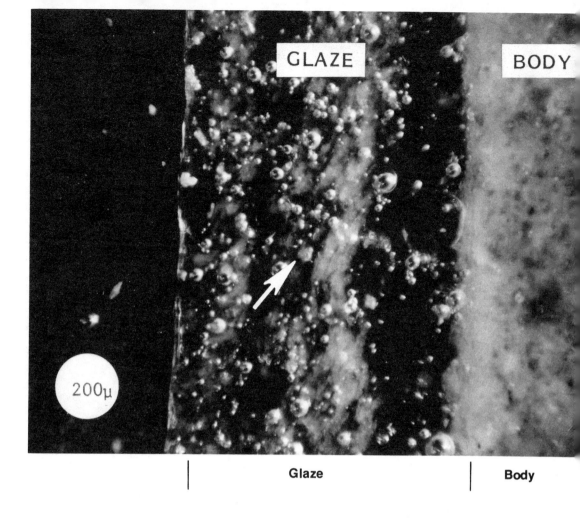

Figure 16.2. Kuan glaze showing undissolved batch. (60 x)

The effect in Kuan pieces is due to two factors: in the first instance, silica and other crystalline ingredients of the glaze are never totally melted or dissolved, hence there is much solid material suspended in the glass (Figure 16.2).

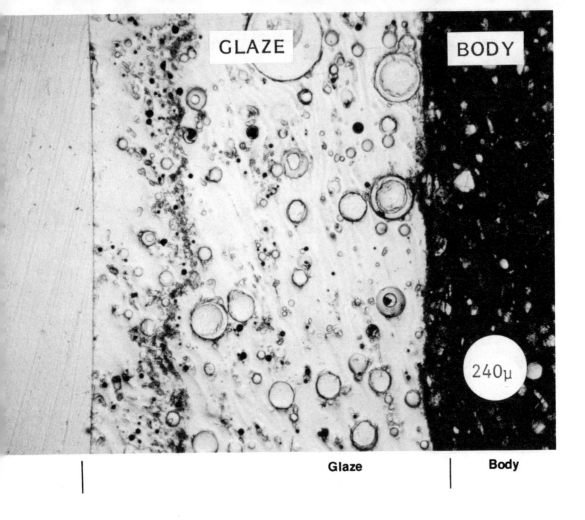

GLAZE BODY

240μ

Glaze | Body

Figure 16.3. Kuan glaze with myriads of bubbles. (50 x)

Secondly, much gaseous matter (air, moisture, and carbon dioxide) is trapped because the glass is never fired high enough to liberate or dissolve it (Figure 16.3).

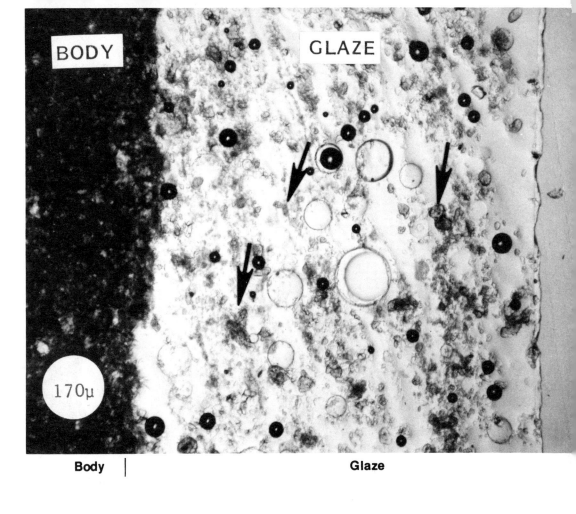

BODY   **GLAZE**

170μ

Body | Glaze

**Figure 16.4. A Lung-ch'uan glaze with bubbles and undissolved silica relicts.
(70 x)**

To a certain degree these phenomena are found in many glazes, but they are most noticeable when the glaze is thick and the firing is decidedly underdone. Lung-ch'uan celadons show much undissolved silica and many bubbles (Figure 16.4) as does Chun ware.

177

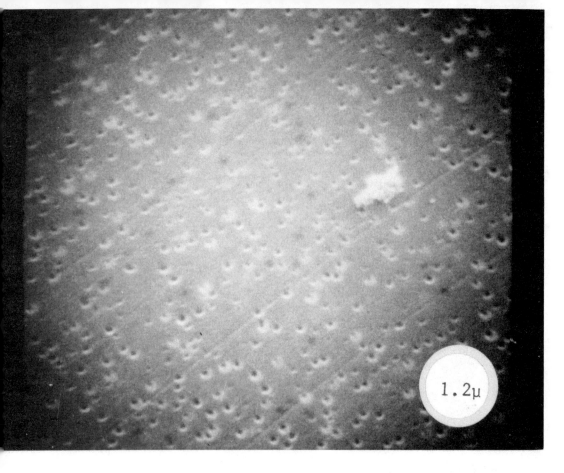

Figure 16.5. A Chun glaze viewed by scanning electron microscopy showing phase separated droplets. (10,500 x)

Chun, in addition, has a type of phase separation that brings a new effect to glazes. This is a liquid-liquid phase separation and is due to a high silica content glaze which also contains a small amount of phosphate. This phosphate (probably from wood-ash) triggers the separation of the glaze into droplets of one glass dispersed in a base of another glass (Figure 16.5).

Where crystals and bubbles in glazes have the effect of making them translucent or white appearing, this true opal in Chun ware also has a coloring effect. Because of the small size of the dispersed droplets ($\sim$ 2000A.), light is diffracted as it passes through the glaze and the result is that it appears brown in transmitted light and blue in reflected light.

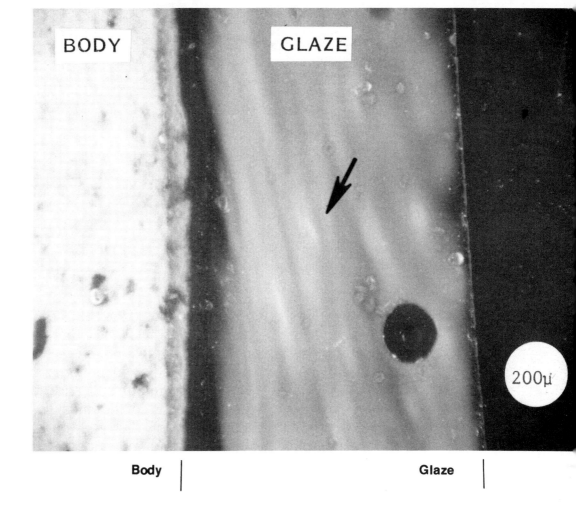

BODY   GLAZE

200μ

Body | Glaze |

Figure 16.6. Chun glaze with opal effect. (60 x)

Since glazes are viewed in reflected light rather than transmitted, this bluish opalescence (Figure 16.6) reinforces the celadon blue of a Chun glaze.

An interesting aspect of liquid-liquid opals is that they can be immediately recognized as such by the eye, even though the particle size of the dispersed phase is too small to be resolved by the optical microscope. The reason for this is that the eye recognizes the optical effects of the droplets rather than the physical appearance of the droplets.

179

This sensitivity of the eye to the brown-blue opal is a very useful test for authenticity in glazes of types other than Chun. When one sees this very fine opalescence in a piece supposed to be of Kuan-type, for example, one's suspicions should be aroused. Kuan glazes are typically underfired and their phase separation is a gross type consisting of bubbles and crystals (Figure 16.3). The liquid-liquid opal on the other hand is a fully fired glaze in which the phase separation appears on cooling. Kuan glazes are so thick that they could never be fully fired without tending to flow off the piece. In Chun ware this flow tendency is quite noticeable.

The reason for suspicion of opalescent Kuan glazes is due to the fact that modern opals are commonly made by the addition of a few percent of fluoride to glazes. This is therefore a quick and easy way to simulate some of the Sung glaze effects. The trained eye, however, rebels at the perfection found in fluoride opals as compared to the imperfect Kuan phase separation. Perfection is really a good reason to reject almost any Sung ceramic. They seem to have had a rare combination of subtle beauty combined with don't-give-a-damn technique.

CHAPTER 17

BODY AND GLAZE RAW MATERIALS

BODY RAW MATERIALS

Body ingredients would seem to be less important than glaze components with regard to overall Sung effects, but this is only partly true. One notices several important points for consideration:

1. Contamination.
2. Background coloration
3. Expansion
4. Translucency
5. Strength
6. Bubbles

CONTAMINATION

The contamination of Sung glazes by the body is frequent. For example examine Chun ware. When the glaze runs thin at the rim, the opalescent color disappears there. This condition is due to extraction of alumina from the body, and that forms a new glaze composition in which phase separation is no longer possible. Now instead of the soft blue Chun color we see at the rim the brownish hue of the body showing through a thin, transparent, glassy layer. A series of analyses shows the reaction which occurs.

Figure 17.1 An EDXR spectrum of the body shows it to be high in alumina.

Figure 17.2 An EDXR of an outer glaze layer illustrates the low alumina content of the original glaze.

Figure 17.3 An EDXR of a glaze layer close to the body demonstrates the movement of alumina from the body into the glaze.

Figure 17.1. EDXR spectrum of Chun body showing
             it to be high in alumina content.

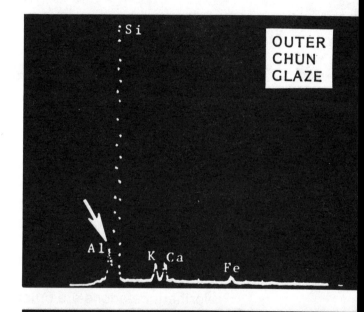

Figure 17.2. EDXR spectrum of outer Chun glaze
             layer illustrating low alumina content
             of original glaze.

Figure 17.3. EDXR spectrum of glaze layer close to
             the body of Chun sherd demonstrating
             the movement of alumina from the
             body into the glaze.

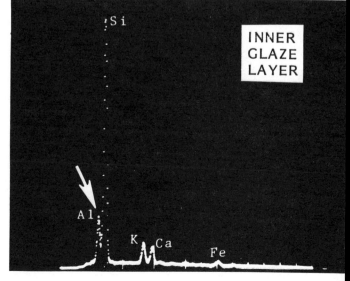

183

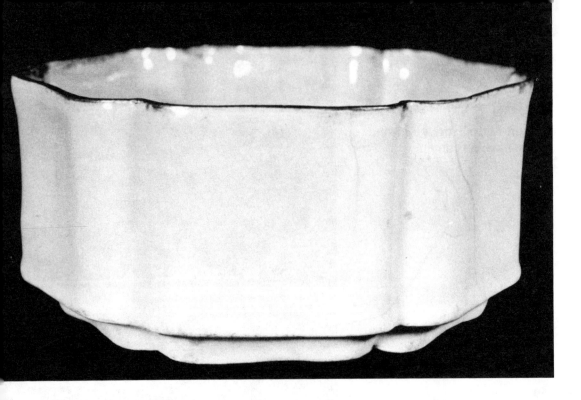

Figure 17.4. Kuan bowl with dark body showing through the pale glaze.

Other examples of glazes contaminated by body material are found in Northern celadons and Lung-ch'uan celadons. Here, in thinner glazes the body influence is due to alumina extraction, as above, plus titania and iron solution. Titania from crude body clays is particularly noted for its browning effect when it interacts with iron and changes its coordination number in the glaze. Northern celadons are outstanding examples of glaze-body reaction because their glazes are thin, highly alkaline (CaO) and high fired. It is this glaze-body reaction that produces the olive and khaki colors that are typical of Northern celadons.

A very subtle body effect can be noted in many Kuan pieces where the dark body shows faintly through the translucent glaze, giving a feeling of great depth. It is almost as if the body and glaze were one substance, uniform throughout, like a piece of jade (which was probably the intended effect). Figure 17.4, a Kuan bowl illustrates this result.

THERMAL EXPANSION

The consequences of body expansion variations in Sung ceramics relate to crazing of the glaze. When this is caused by body situations, we note three categories:

One of these is underfiring. An example is the case of the open pored body that is free to absorb and desorb water, resulting in expansions and contractions that craze the glaze.

Another class of crazing is caused by the physical shape, size, and distribution of body particles. One can readily imagine a body made of coarse clay, coarse feldspar, and coarse flint. If this body were fired to cone 8 a certain expansion would result. However, if the same materials were ballmilled for 24 hours and then fired to cone 8, obviously another expansion would be found.

Finally, much crazing is caused by the chemical makeup of the body. One of the most common ways to correct a low-expansion body is to add crystalline silica to bring up the expansion.

TRANSLUCENCY

Translucency requires fine particle size, appropriate composition (of silica and feldspar), and a high firing temperature for complete fusion. But, translucency is rather moot in the case of Sung ceramics since few examples exhibit this property. Instead, by using thick glazes, Sung potters have implied translucency.

STRENGTH

The strength of bodies has some rather interesting implications. First, one notes that sherd size is related to strength. The thin, porous, weak Kuan bowls produce small sherds, while thick, dense Lung-ch'uan pottery produces large pieces. One wonders what the percentage of survival has been in relation to strength for such ware as Lung-ch'uan with its universally dense body, and Chun ware which frequently had a porous body?

Figure 17.5. Yueh sherd with scribed decoration and a string of bubbles in the glaze. (8x)

BUBBLES

The glaze-body interface is a reaction zone where crystals grow, and where gas bubbles are generated at the nuclei-glaze interface. These are observed frequently in Yueh and Lung-ch'uan ware, especially in the lines of scribed decorations where sharp edges and corners are likely to exist. The strings of bubbles which result are like tiny strings of pearls (Figure 17.5).

GLAZE
RAW
MATERIALS

As noted before, the composition of Sung glazes can be very simple from an ingredient standpoint. For example, it is quite possible to make an acceptable celadon glaze from just pulverized granite and limestone.

While such a glaze has an apparent simplicity, an attempt to duplicate it by using modern raw materials would be complicated. To duplicate a particular granite chemically, one would have to use a mixture of feldspar, silica, iron oxide, and perhaps another balancing ingredient like clay. Then one would have to try and duplicate the particle size of the granite and this would be nearly impossible for a mixture of three or more ingredients.

In addition, since glazes are non-equilibrium systems where reactions are always in the process of occurring, the end result of melting a granite powder would be quite different than melting a mixture of ingredients such as quartz, feldspar, and iron oxide. For one thing, iron oxide is a very active flux in reduction and one would need to duplicate its distribution and chemical binding in order to make a similar glaze.

So once again we must compromise. Our end result must be as close as possible to a Sung glaze, but since there is no way that we can use the exact raw materials we must succeed by knowing our raw materials so well that we can blend them to gain the same effect that the Chinese did. Certainly they had this same problem as they progressed vertically or horizontally through a clay or feldspar deposit. Thus they too knew the frustration of changing raw materials.

To play successfully at this game, we must have a bag of tricks at our disposal. A minimum stock of ingredients would be:

1. Two feldspars (at least) with widely varying potash contents. Hopefully one would be Cornwall stone.

2. Several clays, clean and dirty, coarse and fine, calcined and raw.

3. Two silicas would be nice with different particle sizes.

4. One limestone will be enough, but some calcium phosphate would be useful.

5. There is no apparent difference between ferric oxide and magnetite, but one finds that an ochre or a slip clay is a good source of iron oxide.

With such a palette one can make the substitutions necessary to duplicate the "simple" Chinese glazes.

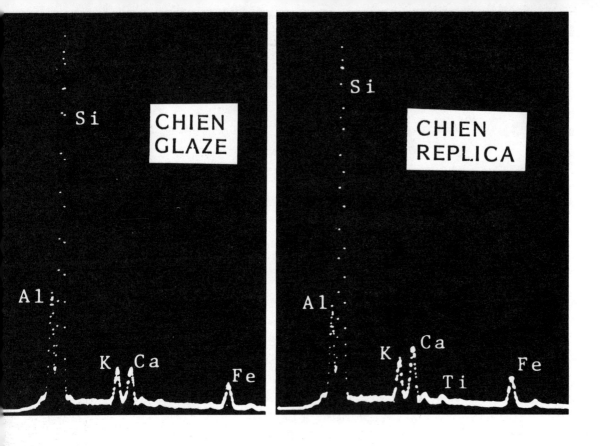

Figure 17.6. EDXR spectra of a Chien glaze and a Chien replica.

ASHES

To the question, "Did Sung potters use wood ash as a common glaze ingredient?" my answer would be an unequivocal **YES.** The strongest answer comes from Chien ware, where synthesis of a glaze using wood ash and a natural clay gave every evidence of being an exact duplicate of the original glaze.

The replicated Chien ware looks like the original both microscopically and macroscopically, and in addition EDXR spectra for both glazes are similar (Figure 17.6).

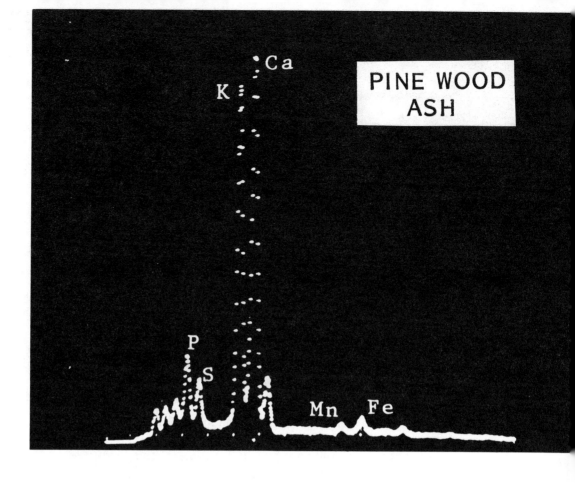

Figure 17.7. EDXR spectrum of Pine wood ash.

Other, less firm evidence comes from the presence of phosphate in Chun, Lung-ch'uan, and Kuan glazes (Sung Sherds", pp. 416 & 439). The concentration of phosphorus is frequently in the neighborhood of 0.5%, which is rather high to attribute to a mineral source like feldspar. On the other hand, it is about right for a wood ash addition.

In formulating my "Chien" glaze, I found that slightly more than 10% wood ash made a good flux content. And in analysing pine wood ash (Figure 17.7) the phosphorus content amounted to a few percent (approximately 5%). Combining these approximations we note that 10% of 5% is 0.5%, or about the range found for phosphorus in Sung glazes.

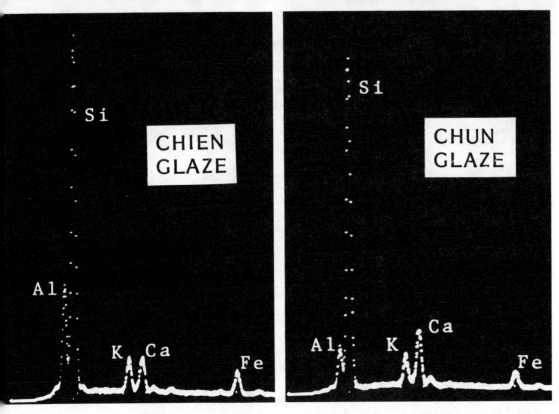

Figure 17.8. EDXR spectra of Chien and Chun glazes.

Another piece of analytical data confirming ash content in Chinese glazes, comes from XRED analysis of Chien and Chun glazes (Figure 17.8). This information has to do with the ratio of potash-to-lime. As can be noted in the above figure, the potash and lime peaks are nearly the same height and are rather low. I have come to conclude that a glaze can be made from such a composition only when ash is used as the glaze flux. If a glaze is made from limestone and potash feldspar to give such a composition, one finds that it is very viscous and hard to melt.

The reason for this is that in a feldspar-containing glaze the potassium is present in little granules of potassium-aluminum-silicate which are very viscous and are not dispersed enough in firing to make a completely homogeneous melt. On the other hand, in wood ash, the potassium is present mainly as potassium carbonate. When this is made into a glaze slip, it dissolves and disperses completely, coating every particle of clay or silica with a layer of flux, whereas the potash in feldspar is only fractionally effective (depending on particle size) in its fluxing ability.

Thus when we see glazes with relatively low contents of potash and lime, as in Figure 17.8, we may assume that they have been made up from wood ash where the fluxing is 100% effective.

GLAZE-ATMOSPHERE INTERACTIONS & GLAZE-BODY INTERACTIONS

REDUCTION

The reaction of glazes with kiln atmospheres is important to this work because many of the Sung pieces have been fired in reduction. It is necessary for us to consider when the reduction took place during the firing operation, and whether this timing is important. It is also useful to determine how much reduction occurred and whether this is a critical parameter.

Fortunately there is one element of reduction firing that we can deal with directly. That is the question of what elements or compounds are doing the actual reduction. If we assume that the Sung Chinese used wood for firing (probably true) then there is the possibility that glaze reduction was caused either by hydrogen, or by carbon monoxide. The answer to this question came early in my glaze testing when I tried making celadons in controlled atmospheres. The results showed that **either** hydrogen or carbon monoxide would produce good results. With the conditions used it was impossible to tell the difference between the two types of reduction from glaze appearance.

We are aided considerably by H.A. Seger's account of firings at the Royal Porcelain Factory in Berlin during the late 1800's. (1).

He carefully described the firing and then analysed kiln atmospheres (Table I) for a number of gases. These firings were made on porcelain using split pine wood as the fuel, so the correlation with Chinese work should be good.

Table I
Gas Analysis from Wood-fired Porcelain Kiln
(Royal Porcelain Factory — Berlin)

Day.	Hour.	Details and observations.	Samples drawn 0.5 m. under the arch.							
			Carbon dioxide.	Carbon monoxide.	Heavy hydrocarbons.	Marsh gas.	Hydrogen.	Oxygen.	Nitrogen.	Per cent. of air.
May 11	A. M. 9.00	Beginning of the burn was at 3 o'clock in the morning, dark red heat - - -	14.0	4.2	0.0	3.4	2.0	0.4	76.0	68
	10.00		15.4	2.7	0.7	2.7	0.0	0.2	78.3	83
	11.00		14.5	3.7	0.4	3.9	0.0	0.0	77.5	65
	12.00		15.3	2.8	0.0	4.0	0.0	0.1	75.8	69
	P. M. 1.00									
	3.30	Fireplace diminished to 50 x 32 cm. by introduction of a firebrick tile - - -	15.1	2.7	0.2	2.2	0.0	0.5	79.3	78
	4.30		17.0	1.7	0.0	2.0	0.6	0.7	78.0	82
	5.30	At the burning down of the last fire - - -								

Porcelain was bluish white, the decoration with cobalt was less pure blue, and in many cases, especially in the thick spots and on the edges of the ware, was bubbled up and sunk in.

(1) The Collected Writings of Hermann A. Seger — Vol. 1. Easton, Pa. 1902, pp. 135-206.

Seger sometimes found hydrogen during reduction, but there was always carbon monoxide present in reduction firing. It is also interesting to note the presence of small amounts of oxygen in this "reducing" atmosphere. This is probably due to incomplete mixing of the gases.

Dr. Seger also comments that it is not necessary to have continual billowing clouds of smoke coming from a kiln in order to ensure complete reduction. And the figures he gives are testimony to this remark.

Seger's statements on the appropriate time for reduction are also helpful. He remarks that the useful time for reduction is in the early stages of firing before the body and glaze have consolidated, and he notes appropriately that an excess of oxygen after the glaze has melted has no effect on the reduced glaze.

His comment on this point leads us to an experiment that everyone should try:

1. Obtain an oxidized, yellow, iron-glazed ceramic. (feldspathic of course).
2. Refire this piece in a strongly reducing kiln to its original firing temperature.

The result will be a yellow, iron glazed ceramic that shows no additional reduction.

Or, the reverse can be tried:

1. Obtain a reduced, green, iron celadon piece.
2. Refire it to its original glazing temperature in a strongly oxidizing atmosphere.

In this case the piece will retain its green celadon color.

The point of each of these experiments is: once a celadon glaze has attained its glassy state, kiln gases do not have a major effect on the oxidation-reduction status of the glaze. There is undoubtedly a slight penetration of a thin surface layer, but this does not affect the basic color of the glaze.

Why is this so? There are two main reasons: first, carbon monoxide does not easily diffuse through glasses because of the large size of the molecule. And hydrogen, which can diffuse through glass, does not have a large driving force such as a pressure difference to force it on. Secondly, iron ions, being di- and tri-valent (with a high polarizing ability) are not prone to diffuse to and from the glaze surface.

If one were to try this same pair of experiments with copper in the reduced and oxidized state, the results would be quite different. This is because of other factors at work. First, copper is volatile at high temperatures in a reducing atmosphere. Second, monovalent copper ions move readily in a molten glass. So our iron experiment is not generally applicable.

This information on glaze-atmosphere reactions is useful to save time and fuel when approaching the end of a celadon firing. When temperature increases are slow it can be advantageous to go oxidizing in order to speed things up.

Of course there is a proper time for reduction of glazes and this occurs when the glaze is porous and yet hot enough for reactions to take place, say from 600° C. to 1000° C. This is also the time to keep the back pressure high in a reducing kiln so that flashing due to air leakage does not occur.

FLAME LENGTH

Another comment by Seger is appropriate at this point. This is on the usefulness of **long** flames in ceramic firing. It is this factor that makes reducing fires very practical in unsophisticated kilns. A long flame, that penetrates to the farthest recesses of a kiln ensures that all parts are at much the same temperature. A short flame on the other hand practically guarantees large temperature gradients. While the high temperature gradients will be smoothed out at the end of a firing, their presence at intermediate stages leads to cracking and distortion problems. Thus, since short flames are tantamount to oxidized firing, we have a second motive for desiring reduction firing.

GLAZE-BODY INTERACTIONS

The reaction between glaze and body in Sung pottery is very significant because of the long firing and cooling schedules necessitated by their kilns. The large kilns with massive saggers and high firing temperatures must have involved firing times in the region of days.

197

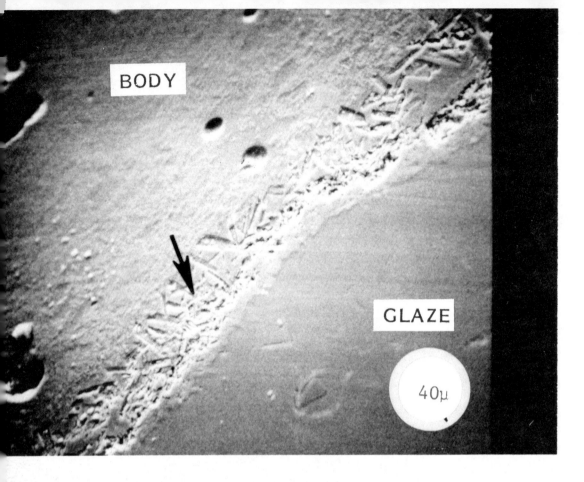

Figure 18.1. Glaze-body interface on Chun ware showing extensive crystallization. (300x)

This long firing and cooling can be confirmed through microscopic examination of at least one glaze, the Chun. There are two clues visible microscopically. First, there are many large crystals (Figure 18.1) at the glaze-body interface. This indicates an extended reaction and a slow cooling process, which by analogy would mean a massive kiln structure and slow firing.

Figure 18.2.

Undissolved silica grain in Chun glaze surrounded by secondary crystals (1000x)

Figure 18.3.

EDXR spectra of secondary crystals showing high silica content.

Second, the undissolved silica grains in the glaze are surrounded by secondary crystals (Figure 18.2) which are also high in silica (Figure 18.3) and are probably cristobalite.

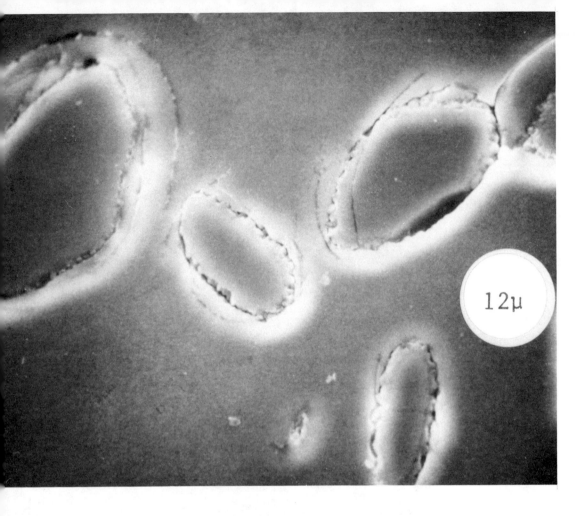

12μ

Figure 18.4. Silica grains in slowly cooled modern glaze showing little second-ary crystal growth. (1000x)

The formation of these secondary crystals also indicates a slow cooling process since an experiment with a similar modern glaze showed much smaller crystals even during an extended cooling cycle (Figure 18.4).

The extensive mullite formation in Sung bodies reported by Sundius (1) is another indication of slow cooling.

To reproduce some of the Sung glaze effects without resorting to exceptional firing and cooling cycles, it becomes necessary to make changes in glaze composition from the originals. The aim is to approach the same final physical and chemical glaze results in a necessarily shorter time. Suggested alterations are:

1. finer particle size raw materials to allow reactions to occur more quickly.

2. An increased lime content (the most reactive ingredient).

3. Slightly higher final temperatures.

These are the type of changes one might make when making a move from a small test kiln to a larger production kiln.

(1) Sung Sherds — Palmgren Sundius and Steger — Stockholm — (1963) — pp. 387-390.

Loading the Kiln.

APPENDIX

Since chemical composition plays such an important role in making Sung-like ceramics, it is appropriate to include some analyses of both raw materials and Chinese ware.

Please use these numbers only as guides though. There is certainly nothing sacred about them, as raw materials will vary from place to place in an ore deposit and we know that glazes will vary from top to bottom and from piece to piece.

RAW MATERIAL ANALYSES

RAW MATERIAL	SiO_2	Al_2O_3	K_2O	Na_2O	CaO	MgO	Fe_2O_3	TiO_2	P_2O_5	LOI
Earth's Crust	59.8	14.9	3.0	3.3	4.9	3.7	6.1	0.8	0.3	—
A Granite	74	13	5	3	1	0.2	3	0.3	0.2	—
A Basalt	52	14.1	1.2	3.2	9.3	6.4	12.8	1.0	0.4	—
A N.Y. Shale	64.6	15.4	3.3	0.6	0.6	2.0	7.2	0.9	—	3.9
Silica Sand	98.5	0.5	—	—	0.3	0.1	0.04	0.01	—	0.1
Cornwall Stone	71.1	16.8	6.6	2.3	1.6	0.1	0.16	0.5	—	1.2
Kona Feldspar A-3	71.6	16.3	7.8	3.7	0.4	—	0.07	—	—	0.1
Buckingham Feldspar	66.3	18.4	11.8	2.7	0.4	—	0.07	—	—	0.3

CLAYS

RAW MATERIAL	SiO_2	Al_2O_3	K_2O	Na_2O	CaO	MgO	Fe_2O_3	TiO_2	P_2O_5	LOI
N. Carolina Kao.	46.1	37.5	0.9	0.2	—	—	0.08	—		14.1
English Kaolin	47.9	37.3	1.9	0.1	0.1	0.1	0.5	0.05	—	12.2
E P K	45.9	38.7	0.2	0.0	0.1	0.1	0.42	0.34	—	14.2
Georgia Kaolin	45.2	38.0	0.0	0.0	0.3	0.3	0.49	1.95	—	13.5
Kentucky Ball	52.1	31.2	1.0	0.3	0.4	0.3	0.8	1.6	—	12.4
Tennessee Ball	53.3	30.1	1.5	0.8	0.3	0.2	1.0	1.4	—	11.4
REDART Clay	64.3	16.4	4.1	0.4	0.2	1.6	7.0	1.1	—	4.8
BARNARD Clay	52.4	10.6	3.8	—	—	—	20.3	0.9	—	8.3 Mn-3.2
Albany Slip Clay	59.5	11.5	2.8	0.4	6.3	3.4	4.1	0.9	—	10.4
Fire Clay	52.0	30.0	0.2	0.1	0.1	0.0	1.0	1.5	—	10.0

ASHES

RAW MATERIAL	SiO_2	Al_2O_3	K_2O	Na_2O	CaO	MgO	Fe_2O_3	TiO_2	P_2O_5	LOI
Pine Wood	24.4	9.7	9.0	3.8	39.7	4.5	3.4	—	2.8	—
Oak Wood	2	—	9.5	3.9	72.5	3.9	—	—	5.8	—
Wheat Straw	66		11.5	2.8	6.1	2.5	—	—	5.4	2.8
Desert Plants	—	—	5.5	28.0	21.1	0.5	—	—	1.8	CO^2-34.0

CHINESE GLAZE ANALYSES

GLAZES	Ref.	SiO_2	Al_2O_3	Fe_2O_3	TiO_2	CaO	MgO	K_2O	Na_2O	P_2O_5	
Ta Yao	SS-33*	68.6	14.3	0.7	0.02	10.4	0.4	5.0	0.1	0.1	
Ta Yao	KX-S3-4**	65.3	16.6	0.8	—	12.2	0.8	3.8	0.5	—	
Yuan Celadon	KX-YL-1	67.4	16.7	1.5	0.14	6.8	0.6	5.5	1.2	—	
Ming Celadon	KX-ML-1	67.6	15.0	1.4	—	6.3	1.7	6.5	1.1	—	
Kuan Celadon	SS-92	63.0	15.3	1.1	0.03	14.5	1.0	4.0	0.2	0.5	
Chun	SS-379	72.8	9.9	1.6	0.07	8.8	1.5	3.9	0.7	0.5	
Chien Temm.	Y&K***	59.8	20.6	6.2	0.65	6.9	2.2	3.0	0.9	—	SO_3-0.6

CHINESE BODY ANALYSES

BODIES	Ref.										
Ta Yao	SS-55	67.4	24.5	2.4	0.18	0.1	0.3	4.5	0.4	—	
Ta Yao	KX-S3-4	61.4	28.0	4.5	0.74	0.9	0.7	3.7	0.4	—	Dark
Kuan	SS-107	64.4	28.7	2.0	1.10	0.3	0.5	2.5	0.2	—	
Yuan	KX-YL-1	70.8	20.1	1.6	0.16	0.2	0.7	5.5	0.8	—	
Ming	KX-ML-1	70.2	20.5	1.7	0.19	0.2	0.3	6.0	1.0	—	
Chun	SS-354	64.9	28.3	2.0	0.9	1.0	0.1	1.9	0.3	—	
Ching Pai	SS-331	77.8	16.2	0.6	0.06	0.4	0.2	3.3	1.1	—	

*SS — Sung St⌐ ⌐.ds, Palmgren
** KX — K'oo-Ku Hsueh-pao, 1973, No. 1, pp 131-156
***Y&K — Oriental Art, XIII, Summer 1967, p. 1 — Yamasaki, K & Koyama, F.

Vogt's Analyses of Ch'ing Raw Materials, Bodies, and Glazes (obtained 1882)

RAW MATERIALS	SiO_2	Al_2O_3	Fe_2O_3	CaO	MgO	K_2O	Na_2O	H_2O	CO_2	CuO	MnO_2	CoO	F
Kaolin	54.55	30.27	0.90	0.27	0.09	2.10	3.82	7.67					
Pe-tun-tze (quartz, Mica)	76.19	16.51	—	0.24	0.11	3.70	0.77	2.34					
Hoa-che (clay, Mica)	47.31	37.74	—	0.26	0.09	3.05	0.82	10.82					
Yeou-ko (quartz, mica)	78.07	13.07	0.90	1.11	tr	2.88	1.18	1.84					
Hoei-yeou (lime, ash)	3.91	1.46	0.49	52.36	0.73	tr	0.25	1.15	37.67				
Tze-kin-che (red clay)	70.00	13.47	8.52	—	0.43	1.58	0.62	4.79					
Leao (cobalt ore)	26.96	36.05	2.42	—	—	0.08	0.34	0.65		1.00	24.61	5.30	

RAW BODIES

	SiO_2	Al_2O_3	Fe_2O_3	CaO	MgO	K_2O	Na_2O	H_2O	CO_2	CuO	MnO_2	CoO	F
Imperial	65.87	22.46	0.76	0.18	—	2.66	2.89	5.49					
Li	65.23	21.97	1.15	0.81	0.11	2.73	1.50	6.50					
Ho	64.65	21.50	1.86	0.15	0.21	3.45	1.19	6.78					
Lin	65.75	21.73	1.03	0.26	0.17	2.66	2.32	6.24					
Body for Cu Turquoise	72.87	17.21	0.96	0.20	0.22	3.97	0.37	4.39					

GLAZES

	SiO_2	Al_2O_3	Fe_2O_3	CaO	MgO	K_2O	Na_2O	H_2O	CO_2	CuO	MnO_2	CoO	F
Celadon	64.77	13.67	1.40	7.50	0.21	2.95	1.98	2.55	5.22				
White	63.40	13.04	0.71	8.76	0.40	3.07	1.93	2.61	6.42				
Bronze	60.89	15.23	3.43	6.72	0.45	2.87	1.40	4.01	5.00				
Blue	63.71	13.02	0.88	6.50	—	2.94	2.31	2.46	5.31	—	—	0.42	
Fine Crackle	72.92	14.98	0.60	1.51	0.15	1.72	5.44	1.62	1.11				
Copper Red	61.57	4.37	0.85	7.43	1.65	5.82	2.86	—	0.80	0.60	PbO 12.71		F 1.75

INDEX

Y

EXPAND YOUR CREATIVE HORIZONS

Salt-Glaze Ceramics
by Janet Mansfield
Discover the techniques of more than 60 ceramic artists currently working with salt glazes in this liberally illustrated offering. You'll garner a wealth of experience as stunning examples of salt-glaze ceramics are brought to life in spectacular color and black-and-white photography.
Hardcover • 8-1/4 x 10-7/8
144 pages
color throughout
SALT • $39.95

Clay And Glazes For The Potter
by Daniel Rhodes
Discover the ins and outs of clay and glazes in this classic work. Rhodes will walk you through Raku, salt firing, fuming with metallic salts, overglaze processes, and the use of fibers and fiberglass in clay. A bonus detailed appendix includes 32 glaze formulas to experiment with.
Hardcover • 8-1/4 x 10-7/8
330 pages
8-page color section
CGFP • $31.95

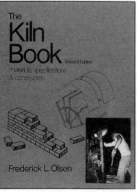

The Kiln Book
2nd edition
by Frederick L. Olsen
You'll find complete plans and instructions for building a kiln of any size and purpose in this informative volume. Plus, discover the principles of efficient design and information on refractory materials, building methods, flues, curved and common walls, bricklaying courses and arches.
Hardcover • 8-1/4 x 10-7/8
291 pages
KILN • $40.00

Electric Kiln Ceramics
A Guide to Clays and Glazes, 2nd edition
by Richard Zakin
This inclusive guide will assist you in using the electric kiln to produce clear, brilliant colors and richly textured surfaces. Provides you with completely revised glaze recipes, information on commercial glaze for low fire and updated health and safety information.
Hardcover • 8-1/4 x 10-7/8
304 pages
16-page color section
EKC2 • $39.95

Raku
A Practical Approach
by Steve Branfman

The Ceramic Spectrum
by Robin Hopper
This is your complete
...uide to materials and
...r testing, mixing, and
...nding. You'll investigate
...specific colors in 134
...ations, all usable in a
... range of tempera-
... and atmospheres.
...cover • 8-1/4 x 10-7/8
...pages
...olor photos
...P • $48.00